Roman and Etruscan Painting

Compass History of Art

Edited by André Held and D. W. Bloemena

The complete series includes:

Roman and Etruscan Painting

Arturo Stenico

of the University of Milan

THE VIKING PRESS
New York

© 1963 by J. M. Meulenhoff Amsterdam

English translation © 1963 by George Weidenfeld and Nicolson Ltd.

Photographs © 1963 by André Held

Translated by Angus Malcolm

A COMPASS BOOKS original edition

Published in 1963 by The Viking Press, Inc.

625 Madison Avenue, New York 22, N.Y.

Library of Congress catalog card number: 63 – 11075

Printed in Holland

Contents

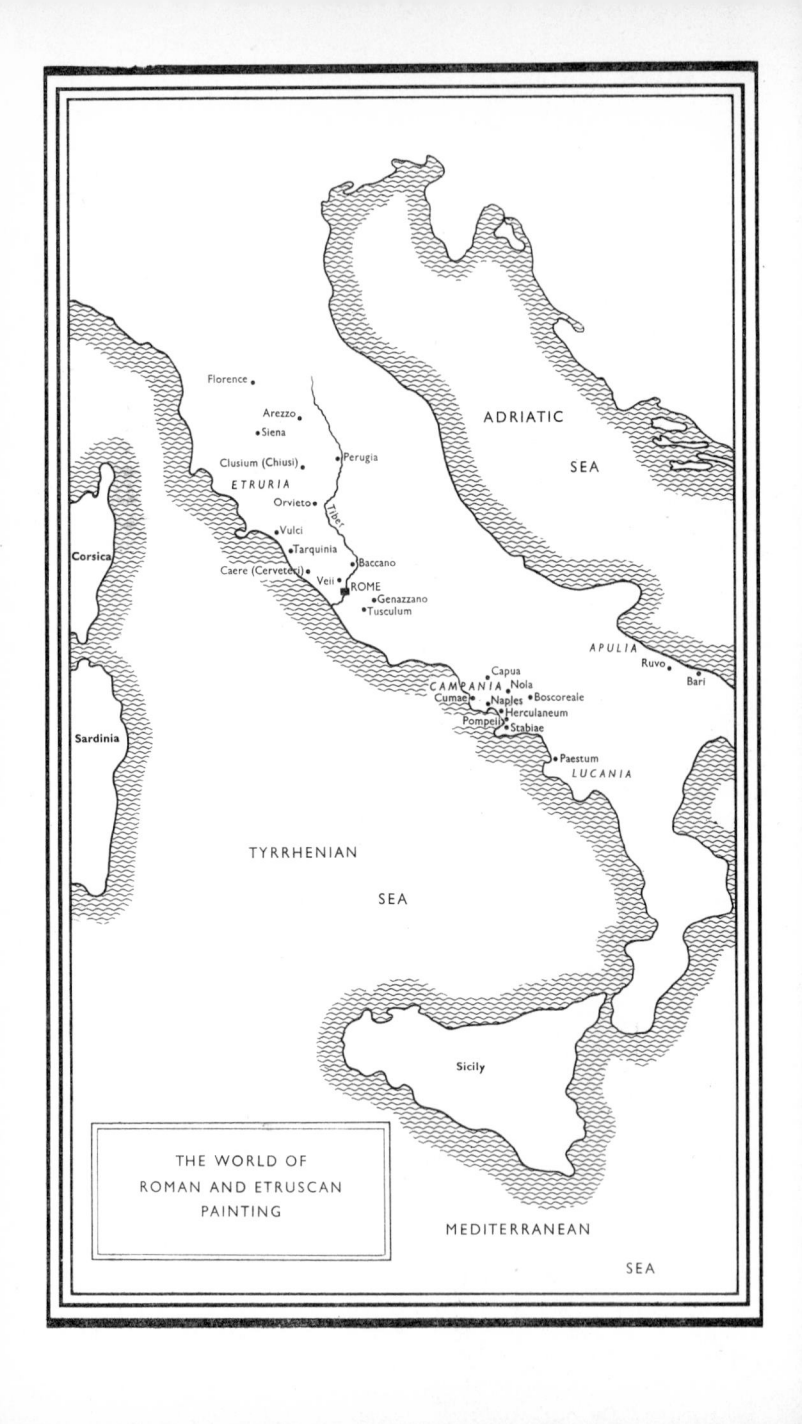

Florence

Arezzo
Siena

Clusium (Chiusi)
Perugia

ETRURIA

Orvieto

Vulci

Tarquinia

Baccano

Caere (Cerveteri)

Veii

ROME

Genazzano
Tusculum

Corsica

Sardinia

ADRIATIC

SEA

APULIA

Ruvo

Bari

Capua

CAMPANIA Nola

Cumae

Naples

Boscoreale

Herculaneum

Pompeii

Stabiae

Paestum

LUCANIA

TYRRHENIAN

SEA

Sicily

THE WORLD OF
ROMAN AND ETRUSCAN
PAINTING

MEDITERRANEAN

SEA

Introduction

An acquaintance with classical art that came only from visits to major museums might well lead anyone to think that it was almost exclusively in sculpture that the ancients—the Greeks, the Etruscans, the Italic peoples and the Romans—expressed their ideals of how to represent people and things. It might also be thought that whether done in marble, stone, terracotta or bronze, ancient sculpture was never coloured. Some excuse for such notions can certainly be found in the present state of our archaeological heritage: all the same, such notions would be seriously wrong.

There is, of course, a great predominance of sculpture in our legacy of ancient figurative art and it overshadows other forms by its quantity alone. Yet painting was an important matter for the peoples of the ancient world, and there is no doubt whatever that it attained the excellence which ancient authors are unanimous in praising. And so great, indeed, was the esteem in which colour was held as an adjunct to *mimesis*, or imitation, that it was regularly applied to buildings, statues and reliefs—sometimes in violent contrasts that make little appeal to our own taste. We must remember, too, that what was painted on a stone statue was not just the borders of the draperies. Conventional colouring was also employed to enhance the realism of some parts of the body. The great religious statues (some of them renowned as marvels) were often 'put together' with ivory and gold or, more modestly, with wood and stone. In other words, there were statues in which flesh and draperies, eyes, hair, armour and attributes were all worked in materials of different kinds and colours, with the colours approximating (within certain conventions) the real colours of the things represented. Moreover a bronze statue which has eyes of vitreous paste or semi-precious stone and nipples adorned with copper foil proves that the artist was not satisfied with the degree of life which modelling and its effects of light and shade could give to his work.

But although there are a few cases in which the soil has yielded statues and reliefs that show faint remains of colouring, we do not possess a single one of the great paintings of antiquity that are celebrated in the written texts we know. Nor can this grievous loss be remedied, although experts have tried—sometimes with conflicting results—to detect some echo of these vanished pictures in decorations of inferior quality and much later date which may perhaps derive from them. The perishable nature of the materials the painters used (the wooden panels or the pigments themselves) and the destruction of buildings with decorated walls—these are among the main things that explain why we do not possess a single one of the works that the ancient writers praise or describe, nor even a fragment of painting that can be ascribed to a single one of the many masters of the brush and stylus who are listed or mentioned by the ancients.

In contrast with this absolute lack of originals we have an enormous number of names and 'titles' of pictures and paintings that were prized in antiquity. These lists, moreover, must themselves be regarded as very incomplete since they derive from sources that were influenced by the taste of the period in which they were compiled, or by the taste of the period in which the writer lived from whose works they were derived. Most of the written sources refer to Greek painting, or rather to Greek painters, of the fourth century BC or of the Hellenistic age; and this fact disposes of another delusion entertained even by well-known experts, *viz.* that while the Greek achievement was above all in plastic art it was the inhabitants of the Italian peninsula who discovered the world of colour and thus gave Western civilization the art of painting. The truth is that while the majority of works of sculpture are either of directly Greek origin or are easily classified as copies of Greek originals (especially between the fifth century BC and the late Hellenistic period), it is in the soil of Italy that the largest quantity of ancient painting has survived, even though the paintings are not the ones which the ancient writers mention and cannot be attributed to the artists those writers name. Nevertheless, the inhabitants of the Italian peninsula cannot, to a greater degree than those of the Greek or of the Greek world at large, be credited with an intense or widespread vocation for the world of colour simply because it is in their area that the bulk of ancient painting has been preserved. This preservation is due to causes that have nothing to do with aesthetic values or even with the original quantity of painting. The real reason why we can still see in Italy one of the most complete series of wall-paintings (even though a large number of them is lost) lies in the burial-rites practised by the Etruscans, which differed in several respects from those of the Greeks. And it is merely to a seismic convulsion that we owe the preservation, with so many other artefacts, of one outstandingly valuable group of late Hellenistic and Roman paintings—those which once adorned the walls of the buildings that were buried by the dramatic eruption of Vesuvius in AD 79.

Etruscan Painting

General Characteristics

The largest number, and the best, of the Etruscan paintings we know were made on the walls of the chamber-tombs cut in the rock beneath the necropolises—large in themselves and often impressive, even outside —that adjoin the main cities of southern and central Etruria. Although this type of painting is abundant and provides the student with a fairly continuous series of examples from a variety of Etruscan centres, it should at once be made clear that the surviving funerary paintings are no more than a pitiful remnant of what once existed. All we have of that immense inheritance is a selection made, once again, by chance; for the mere discovery of what has been preserved underground was for the most part the result not of systematic exploration of the burial areas but of accident and empirical methods. New techniques are now available for examining the sub-soil—specially designed apparatus and ingenious instruments for inspecting the interior of funeral-chambers when identified—and these have recently provided new and important examples of Etruscan funerary painting, many of them still unpublished. The Tomb of the Olympiads, some details of which are given in figures 17–19, is the most noteworthy fruit of this technique of exploration. No modern technical device, however, can restore to us the paintings that have disappeared—either as a result of natural causes such as humidity or subsidence, or through looters who in the course of so many centuries have rifled tombs and then left them exposed to the destructive forces of nature: changes of climate, erosion and so forth. Even in tombs that have been opened, not by sacrilegious thieves but by eager antiquarians, a large part of the paintings has completely vanished or has suffered irreparable damage. A painted tomb, once opened, is a prey to the fluctuations of temperature, atmospheric pressure and humidity that take place outside but were gradual and limited inside so long as the tomb was sealed off from the atmosphere. The colours then fade, the plaster flakes and the surface of the rock disintegrates. The sole remedy for these calamities is to detach the paintings, consolidate them and transfer them to canvas stretched on a special frame. In the years following the war the skilled technicians of the Central Institute for Restoration carried out a number of these operations, and thus saved paintings whose condition was already so serious in some cases that they would otherwise have completely disappeared.

It is, of course, less exciting to see tombs nowadays that have been reconstructed in the air-conditioned setting of museums than it is to expose oneself to the revelation of Etruscan painting by descending uncomfortably into the bowels of the earth, with the outlines of the hills and woods that surround the ancient necropolis still fresh in the mind's eye. But the removal of the paintings will, one hopes, preserve them for the eyes of future generations too. If so, any lack of romantic surroundings will be amply compensated for. In any case, a large proportion of the painted tombs still awaits removal from the necropolises. Every time the need arises to give a survey of Etruscan painting in photographs the expert is in difficulty. A number of tomb-paintings, including some of outstanding importance and quality, are today in a lamentable state even if they have not entirely disappeared. We can study these only by means of water-colours, drawings, tracings and engravings that were made before photography was invented or before it formed part of an archaeologist's equipment. As records these are of uneven value, although priceless for the expert who can assess and interpret them with a philological eye; but they cannot be used with impunity in a non-technical essay on Etruscan painting. Not even old photographs taken when the damage was less extensive than it is today (though depressing enough even then) can be reproduced without apology, save in a learned publication. It is, for these reasons, impossible to present a complete or systematic set of illustrations of even the most notable Etruscan tomb-paintings; and the gaps that exist are all the more serious because even in the better-preserved tombs a good part of the pictorial decoration has vanished altogether, or has been spoiled by damage (or sometimes by unavoidably necessary restoration) or else is in such a condition as to discourage the experienced photographer—as the present writer can testify—from wasting any time on it. What is offered here is therefore a selection of subjects, general views and details, made *faute de mieux*.

Nor, it must be pointed out, is there any means of adequately illustrating decoration which normally runs right round the walls of a funeral chamber. In consequence, it is not possible to illustrate fully the composition and decorative value of the pictures which the artist created, or to show his conception of the general lay-out of the scenes which he was painting; and this fact also makes the theme of the paintings look episodic and disjointed.

But in spite of all this we do possess an abundant and continuous series of wall-paintings in Etruscan territory and it extends through several centuries—from the end of the seventh to the first century BC.

There are very few branches of art in the ancient world for which as much can be claimed. In this respect the necropolis of Tarquinia is outstanding in that several dozen painted tombs, including some that exist no more, are known to us from the records of travellers and archaeologists who, in the course of the past three centuries and a half, have traversed the great city of the dead to visit them. It is not only on account of the latest discoveries that Tarquinia, even today, retains the primacy in the field of funerary painting, for the examples there are abundant and they cover the greater part of the history of Etruscan painting. But other centres also present us with more or less isolated examples: Clusium (Chiusi) in the first place, and then Orvieto and Vulci, Veii (Veio) and Caere (Cerveteri). Further places, too, are known as the sites of tombs now lost. All this goes to show that the practice of painting funeral chambers was not restricted to one centre or to a single limited area but was widespread enough for us to call it typically Etruscan.

The remarkable extent to which Etruscan civilisation has, in our eyes, a funereal character is due to the fact that its remains come chiefly from burial-places or were conceived and made for the use of the dead. The ground-plan of the tomb and its architecture were determined by the Mediterranean belief that this was where the life of the departed would continue—a life *sui generis*, yet attended by needs like those of life on earth; and for the convenience of the dead in their new and permanent home there arose both the need of equipping it with what was requisite (the so-called funeral furniture) and the opportunity of adorning it with paintings. Occasionally, but only in the most archaic period, these paintings were purely decorative and it is unlikely that figure-designs, such as those in the Boccanera slabs, were intended to recall episodes in the earthly life of the departed. Episodes drawn from Greek mythology are rare in the earlier periods. In the great majority of cases the walls of Etruscan tombs are painted with scenes from real life at its gayest and most carefree, with pleasant sights and moments of rejoicing; dances alternate with music and are interspersed with athletic games and spectacles, with hunts and pleasures on the water. Most prominent of all, and not in numbers alone, are the banquets and the *symposia*. In these paintings, designed to re-create surroundings of real life and earthly pleasures for the departed, there is probably a magico-religious intention. Death itself, when touched on, appears as a thing that happens on earth among the living—an incident, one might say, of daily life. All these remarks apply to the series of Etruscan funerary paintings of the archaic and post-archaic periods. With the fourth century (and the evidence comes not only from paintings) there appears a weakening of the belief that the dead live in the tomb as in their home; instead, there is belief in an unearthly place where men meet—a kind of Greek Hades. The shades of the departed are henceforth in an imaginary world, a murky world devoid of earthly pleasures, a world often stormy, in which monstrous shapes appear through the mists. All this is very different in spirit from the representations of Hades in the art of Greece where, unless mystical influence is more or less explicit, the world beyond the grave is a mythological one. Even in some Etruscan paintings the element of Greek mythology is recognisable in characters involved in the magical funerary rites or, in general, in those of Avernus; but this element is mixed up with the macabre inventions of Etruscan demonology. Yet even when the fearsome demons are absent and the functions of the Fates are limited to tearing the dead away from their dear ones, and even when the dead man is honoured in the Beyond by the presence of Aita (Hades) and Phersipnai (Persephone), the rulers of the underworld—even then the sorrow of the departed is plain and the mourning of the relatives unmistakable.

It was naturally for the upper and richer social class that these sumptuous funeral monuments were built and decorated, and this is true of every period in Etruscan painting; but in the later tombs we can feel pretty sure that one of their objects was to flatter the aristocratic pride of certain noble Etruscan families. The dead are shown banqueting, and in the very latest period of painting there is a tendency to give their faces the individual character of a portrait, *i.e.* to make them identifiable in the picture itself, whereas in the earlier period a figure was identified by an accompanying inscription. The world revealed to us by these funerary paintings is a world of rich and powerful men; but the most modest urns (often made in quantity, or in moulds) show that the same mentality and the same beliefs prevailed in the lower classes too.

As a rule, the burial-chamber is architectonically treated as though it formed part of a house. A flight of steps leads through a door into a rectangular space into which—in the most elaborate kinds—open other chambers, axially or laterally arranged. The roof is made to slope on either side from an imitation central beam, and this fiction results in two walls (usually the entrance-wall and the one opposite) terminating overhead in a wide isosceles triangle, a pedimental space, with a central carved vertex, in the middle of which a false corbel supporting the *columen* (or top of the pediment) is very often painted. In some cases (for example in the Tomb of the Monkey at Clusium) the roof is treated three-dimensionally and represents a structure of a most unusual kind, albeit of architectonic derivation. The openings are normally treated as doors, with the posts and lintel indicated in paint. Fairly common, too, are false doors, painted to represent wood with metal bosses.

Painting on anything but walls is exceptional: it occurs on a few stone sarcophagi and a few terracotta urns.

In view of the abundance and the organic character of the documentation provided by wall-painting, it would be natural—and would not be too serious a loss—if we were to overlook the examples of true and essentially Etruscan decoration that come from other sources: from the designs painted on various kinds of vase or engraved on metal mirrors or on other objects decorated in relief.

The Main Centres

Caere and Veii are the centres which hitherto have yielded the oldest examples of Etruscan painting, but there is no reason to suppose that painting was not practised at other places at the same period.

In the Tombs of the Painted Animals and of the Painted Lions, both at Caere, there are a few half-obliterated remains of wall-paintings that transport us to the fabulous world of purely decorative painting. Oriental in origin, they belong to a time in which the religious meaning of some subjects had been forgotten even in the places where the style evolved. The troops of animals, mostly exotic and feline, the 'King of beasts', the palmettes, the conventional colouring which emphasises the highly stylised anatomy and structure—all these are elements of an 'Oriental' decorative style which, starting from the shores of the Aegean and the easternmost part of the Mediterranean, spread widely in Etruria. It appears on objects made of precious metals, on the ordinary painted pottery and, although no example has been discovered, in the decoration of textiles which were imported in quantity from those areas during the seventh century BC. The fashion for these imported objects led to the creation and popularity of Italic imitations. But this very interesting period of Etruscan art is not at all worthily represented by the tomb-paintings mentioned above, which can be assigned to the final phase of this first florescence among the archaeological 'finds' in Etruria.

Probably later in date is the painting which decorates the end-wall of the first chamber in the Campana tomb at Veii. Its frieze of superimposed panels is archaic as regards the strongly-marked equality in the height of the heads yet 'Oriental' in its design, which is composed of figures and foliage intertwined and interlaced. Both elements are highly stylized in outline and in colour, and the foliage, for conventional and decorative reasons, is evenly used in each part of the design. The whole forms a kind of large tapestry hanging on either side of the door and in type and style it shows close contact with the 'Daedalic' phase of Cretan art. Experts have discussed at length the most complex part of the frieze, which is fairly well visible in drawings and old photographs, in the hope of being able to explain the subject. Most likely it is a hunting scene in the 'Oriental' manner; but uncertainty persists, because the painter was more concerned with decoration than with telling a story.

Graeco-Oriental Influence

There is no doubt, on the other hand, that story-telling was the purpose of the five Boccanera slabs—so called after their discoverer—which are now in the British Museum. They were found in the necropolis of Caere and belong to a single series. For the reason, among others, that the parts recovered are most unlikely to constitute the whole decoration of the tomb, it is not easy to explain the subject which three of them represent. One of the persons shown wears the dress of an Etruscan priest, and there are other attributes which may be considered local. But it is still a matter for discussion whether we have here a record of a royal ceremony or the story of an Etruscan myth not otherwise known to us. Even the stylistic threads that go back to the Hellenic world, though plain enough in a general way, are not easy to identify in the tapestry presented by the frieze. They include features found on Corinthian pottery; but other ingredients, of a kind we can broadly call Graeco-Oriental, are none the less present—in the repertory of human figures, in the drawing of anatomical details, or in characteristics of dress. But rising above all these imported elements and fusing them with the spontaneity of popular art is a common factor—primitive, clumsy but lively—which cannot be other than Etruscan. Two of the slabs show a heraldically couchant sphinx which fills the whole depth of the frieze. It is very likely that these two slabs flanked the door and that the dimorphic creatures which they represent served as guardians of the tomb. Even though its type is familiar, the sphinx (fig 1) with the raised claw is one of the most satisfying features of this series of paintings. Its body is geometrically rendered in curved surfaces and outlines; it fits, un-cramped and un-distorted, into its field and fills it with completeness and precision. Its ample wing is unfolded with a lively decorative sense, in a volute that might have been drawn with a compass; the feathers are highly stylised and the limited range of their colouring is repeated, with a simple but highly ornamental rhythm, in a balanced pattern. The swirl of the wing and the upward lines of the claws counterbalance the sinuous movement of the black and quivering tail. The head is massive, with a harsh profile and jaw erect on a lengthy neck. The straight line of the nose and brow and the great eye shown in full are typically archaic in general; but here they have something unusual, something we are justified in calling peculiar to Caere.

Certain other panels, now in the Louvre, known as the Campana slabs from the name of their former owner (although tradition says they came from the necropolis of Caere) must be assigned to a later date. Considerably restored, they belong to two series of narrative paintings whose subjects, once again, are still uncertain. The Campana slabs can be related to the Boccanera ones not only on account of their common origin and their identical technique but also by the coincidence of a certain number of stylistic features. But their more delicate and sophisticated rendering of persons in various attitudes makes these pictures less vivid, less 'Etruscan', than the rather coarser ones in the British Museum. They can be dated to the middle of the sixth century BC and are more or less contemporary with some other slabs (or parts of slabs) from Caere that were recently discovered. Although these were found as a number of minute fragments and are still incomplete after restoration, two of them undoubtedly show in outline the representation of a Greek myth: the slaying of a Gorgon by Perseus. The three monstrous figures of the Gorgons have survived: they are hairy of body and lively even in their stereotyped movements, and a great decorative sense is shown in the play of the intertwined serpents that surmount their full-faced, roundish visages. The lesser frieze, almost miniature in scale, which runs along the top, is also of unusual interest in so far as it can still be made out.

Other slabs from Caere, more or less coeval with these, have been found outside the necropolis, for example, in the Temple of Hera. Though sadly fragmentary, these are specimens of non-funerary Etruscan painting. But from what can be seen of them, they do not exhibit any difference of tone or style from the examples of Caere painting of the second half of the sixth century BC that have been revealed to us by the tombs.

Though Caere is the place that has yielded the most important, as well as the largest, group of Etruscan paintings from the earliest period, the real museum of Etruscan painted tombs is the necropolis of Tarquinia. There, preserved and recorded, we have a rich series, chronologically almost complete, of Etruscan painting as it developed after the middle of the sixth century BC.

With the paintings of the Tomb of the Bulls (figs 2–4) we are not far removed in time from the Boccanera slabs; and, despite the physical separation of the two centres of art, we can plainly see certain elements in the Tarquinia paintings that were present, though subordinate and perhaps not fully developed, in those of Caere. In the Tomb of the Bulls we find for the first time a complete scheme, well preserved and free from serious gaps. The principal picture is on the wall opposite the main entrance-door, between two openings which lead into two inner and smaller chambers. The subject is taken from Greek mythology. In a thicket behind a monumental fountain, Achilles waits in ambush for Priam's young and rather effeminate son, Troilus. The latter is unarmed save for a goad, and is leading a horse to water. The point of the incident lies in the contrast between brutal excitement on the one hand and gentle, unsuspecting calm on the other. The incident is one which, with repetitions and variations, was constantly treated in the archaic art of Greece. But the Tarquinia 'picture' is not just a copy, truncated at that, done by an Etruscan artist whose lack of skill in drawing can be seen at various points, especially in the long legs of the horse. If the painter had anything to copy it was no more than some aids to memory, and he found himself driven to invent a composition of his own in order to fit the various ingredients into his picture. It was almost too simple to balance the design by planting a large palm tree in the middle so as to make two equal spaces, each roughly square. Yet *horror vacui* is not the only thing to which we should ascribe the abundance of plant-motifs in the background—the vine-tendrils and the thickets, and the other features included either for their decorative value or as part of the setting of the incident. In this picture they seem to foreshadow that love of nature which was to be so prominent in painting at Tarquinia later on. Although influences from other quarters not easily identified are perceptible, it is the Ionic-Asiatic elements which predominate here. In the flaccid rendering of the young man's body with its concave back, in the thin and wavering outline of his elongated head (its elliptical shape emphasised by the way the hair is worn), in the type of lion cub crouching on top of the fountain, we have the essential characteristics of this painting; and they enable us to fit it with confidence into the varied series of Etrusco-Ionic works belonging to other branches of art.

This Ionic strain is still more obvious in the groups painted on the long band that runs above the door and the picture of Achilles and Troilus. Free from architectonic constriction, these two groups (whose indecency, alas, prevents their illustration) are done on a miniature scale without visual confusion and they reveal one of the characteristics of Etruscan art by their immediacy, their vivacity and their capture of realistic detail. In one of them a bull lies peacefully stretched out, his round eyes fixed in a bovine stare; in the other, which is intricately patterned, a bull with a human head (fig 4) is charging. The composite nature of the bull detracts not at all from the naturalism which the painter has achieved with limited means and with extreme simplicity of freehand drawing. The designs painted on the pediment are less successful but are certainly by the same hand. The evidence lies in their affinity with types already common (for example, the chimaera stopped by a horseman whose original must have been Bellerophon) and in the obvious awkwardness of the composition that resulted when the painter had to fit his material into a triangular space.

The Tomb of the Bulls, which is perhaps a little later than its style may suggest, is the earliest of the archaic and post-archaic painted tombs at Tarquinia—a series which has been fairly well recorded. It is also the only tomb of its period in which mythological themes predominate. As we pass to the more recent tombs we no longer see the fabulous deeds of the heroes but the real world of the Etruscans—the exuberance of their life at feast-times, with indications of their rites and their beliefs.

The Tomb of the Augurs at Tarquinia (figs 5–9) devotes the greater part of its space to scenes of athletic games and spectacles; but the end-wall, by tradition the most important, is reserved for an elaborate composition dealing with a stage in the funeral rites. Here we behold two male figures in hieratic poses that combine respect with deep but muted sorrow (figs 8 and 9). They appear on each side of a door which is painted on the centre of the wall and which, if not meant for the real door of Hades, represents at any rate the door that closes the sepulchre. What is perhaps a more human sign of sorrow, seen freshly and without too much concern for the balance of the composition, is to be found in the small crouching figure, enveloped in a cloak, which is painted on the right-hand wall near the corner where it meets the end-wall (fig 7). The whole of the rest of the decoration, however, is an exuberant display of vitality and movement. Potential movement is represented by the two wrestlers whose ponderous bodies converge obliquely and divide the wall (fig 5). Elsewhere, movement becomes explicit in the gesticulations of the persons in sumptuous clothes who are watching the match. The *agonothetes* (a kind of umpire) was wrongly interpreted by early students as an augur (partly on account of the proximity of flying birds) and thus gave the tomb its name. The right-hand wall ends with another scene of movement which has greatly interested students, especially on account of its antiquarian aspects. It shows a sanguinary incident which has been thought a forerunner of the gladiatorial contests that so fascinated the public several centuries later (fig 6). A personage wearing a head-piece, peaked and strangely adorned, and clothed in a tight-fitting spotted jerkin, holds a ferocious dog on a long leash. The dog is attacking a half-naked man whose head is entirely wrapped in a white cloth. Thus blindfolded, he tries to defend himself with a club against the dog whose fangs have already drawn blood from his legs; but the leash entangles his limbs and impedes his movements so that he seems to be in serious straits. The man who is setting the dog at him appears to be masked, and in the painted inscription alongside he is designated as *phersu*—a term which experts relate to the Latin *persona* and read as meaning 'masked man'. This personage is of an undoubtedly local type and he reappears, as the only recognisable figure, on the opposite wall of the tomb, where he is shown apparently in flight. The episode of the *phersu* and the blindfolded man was, incidentally, found again not long ago, though in a sad state of preservation, on the walls of the Tomb of the Olympiads.

Ionic Influence

The Tomb of the Augurs shows the full impact of Ionic influence in the heavy, rounded heads, the powerful, fleshy limbs, the shaved upper lip on the bearded faces, and the decorative treatment of such anatomical details as the ears. These are some of the features which show the extent to which the Graeco-Oriental school of painting dominated southern Etruria in the second half of the sixth century BC. It is above all to certain pieces of a special type of pottery — the so-called *hydrie* (or water-pots) of Caere — highly interesting for many reasons, that the specialists often refer when studying the style of this tomb. And, indeed, in the naked bodies of the wrestlers, which are charged with brute force on the point of release, it is easy to see references to Hercules, whose deeds seem to have been favourite subjects of the painter of the Caere water-pots. That painter was certainly a Greek from the coast of Ionia. Nevertheless, in these vase-pictures (the term 'pictures' is justified by the range of colours used) there predominates a spirit of irony, almost of caricature, which is absent—so far as we know—from the other kinds of painted pottery of Oriental origin or Ionic inspiration. All the same, we cannot, of course, expect to find this irreverent spirit in a funerary painting. The man who painted the Tomb of the Augurs was an Etruscan, one who derived his formulae and style from the then dominant Ionic manner and yet was able to indulge that taste for narrative and for realistic detail which forms no mean part of the Etruscan artistic spirit. The naturalistic elements too, the flora and fauna (young shoots and sprays of bell-shaped flowers, and birds), though sparsely used, provide further grounds for classifying a painting as Etruscan.

To the same period belongs the Tomb of the Lionesses at Tarquinia (figs 10–13), though it is of slightly later date, like the Tomb of the Inscriptions and the Tomb of the Dead Man. Both of these are at Tarquinia but their decoration is very poorly preserved. The plan of this tomb is the same as that of the one described above. On the pediment of the end-wall are painted two feline beasts, plainly female (fig 11), which have given the tomb its name. Here the general scheme of composition is reversed as compared with the Tomb of the Augurs: except in a few places, the side-walls are treated statically. Large-scale figures of banqueters are shown recumbent on the *kline*, or couch (see, for example, fig 10) and they are watching the lively spectacle which the artist has painted on the end-wall with such a mature sense of composition and such acute observation. The spectacle is one of music and dancing that takes place on each side of a great two-handled *krater*, or bowl, garlanded with Bacchic ivy. The banquet is set indoors, and the roof is supported by columns that make partitions for the decoration. In this picture, therefore, we should not expect to find those elements of landscape and foliage that we saw in the Tomb of the Augurs and shall continue to find in later paintings. Nevertheless, this is one more tomb in which we sense the painter's love for the animal world and his desire to widen his horizons, however incongruously; the evidence is found in the band that runs below the narrative frieze and shows the undulant surface of the sea, over which dolphins and little flying sea-birds dart in an endless and unvarying rhythm. But this band occupies a minor place in the general scheme of composition, which is dominated by the large patches of strong, bright colour in the major frieze. A powerful impression is made by the figures of men in motley clothing who recline on vari-coloured cushions, holding cups and other objects, in poses that leave the close-knit design intact. These figures reveal once more the Ionic traits to which we have repeatedly drawn attention (fig 10). Their profiles and the way their hair is dressed remind us of two well-known terracotta sarcophagi from Caere—one in the Villa Giulia Museum and the other in the Louvre—each of them a real masterpiece of Etruscan plastic art in the Ionic manner. These figures in the round possess, moreover, the selfsame majesty we see in the pose of the figures who take part in the banquet. The comparison provides a further proof of how widespread was the Ionic-Etruscan style.

But it was on the end-wall of the Tomb of the Lionesses that this painter's personal style found its happiest expression. Flowing lines and abundant colour create lively and varied rhythms, and are controlled by simple, well-concealed principles of composition that correspond, more-over, to the two different aspects of the subject treated. The figures are engaged in several kinds of dance. (It should not be thought that these are taking place simultaneously—a warning that applies also, for example, to the gymnastic games in the Tomb of the Augurs and in later tombs.) The nature of the dance is shown primarily by the instrument that accompanies it. The double flute on the right launches the young couple into an orgiastic movement—a little ragged and not quite 'in time' (fig. 12). They are wholly engrossed in their wine-dance, as it might be called: the fair-haired young man with the pitcher is nude, while the dark-haired girl with the pale skin wears a cape. From the roof hangs a long-handled *simpulum* (or ladle) and in the corner a dark pool issues from another pitcher standing on the ground. To the sound of a zither, a female dancer swathed in rich and elaborate garments, her hair bound high on her head in a *tutulus*, moves majestically leftwards; her step is long, and the movement of her arms and outspread hands is most expressive. This dance is a slow one, almost 'classical'—the very opposite of the wild and rustic dance of the couple painted beyond the *krater*, which thus serves to mark an interval between the two kinds of music. The drawing is very delicate and one detail is enough to show the artist's powers in this respect: the small figure of a youth (fig. 13) is shown in a simple silhouette drawn with a sinuous line that reveals no sign of those corrections which are so common in other figures of this period. The colour-scheme of the decoration in this tomb is very bright and attrac-tive. In the Tomb of the Augurs, the dominant colours are black, white and red in various shades, while blue and green are used only sparingly; but the Tomb of the Lionesses shows a wider range. Its colours are used over larger areas: they are sharply but not disagreeably contrasted and are skilfully balanced within a composition that reveals careful discipline.

This great vivacity is enhanced by the colour but does not overpower the delicate patterns of the embroidered stuffs or of the ornamental band (composed of alternating palmettes and lotus-buds) that runs between the two friezes. In the dark recesses of the sepulchre the colours 'sing' as if they were lit up by the sun itself.

A comparable effect of lively colouring is to be found on the walls of the second chamber in the Tomb of the Hunt and Fishing—one of the strangest examples not merely of Tarquinian or even of Etruscan painting in general, but of all archaic classical art (figs 14–16). On the almost-faded walls of the first chamber, the little figures that dance and make music are separated by trees hung with wreaths, necklaces, ornaments and other objects. As far as one can still make them out, the designs are lively and varied; and here for the first time we observe the device (very popular afterwards) of using little trees to divide up the composition into a series of more or less equal panels in which the persons of the decoration are placed. Here, too, it is to be noted that in relation to the surrounding foliage the human figure, if not exactly secondary, is not at all predominant. More traditional in its scheme and in its conventional colouring is the crowded scene of the return from the hunt, which fills the pediment in the first chamber; the bushes are highly stylized and their function is rather to fill up space than to suggest a landscape. The animals (especially the dogs) are drawn in natural attitudes which do not, however, go beyond the already established Etrusco-Ionic tradition.

There is no less crowding, though more skilful planning, in the composition which occupies the pediment in the inner room (fig 14). It represents a couple on a *kline*, surrounded by servants and musicians; the central group is badly damaged but its remains are majestic in design and gain much from the women's rich and heavy garments. The subject is typical of this phase of Etruscan painting, and its narrative character is shown in the attitudes of the servants—especially in the humble posture of the two maids with the wreaths at the foot of the *kline*.

Nature and Realism

The main interest of the pictorial scheme lies, however, in the uninterrupted frieze that covers the walls of the second chamber with scenes —some on the sea and some on the rocks rising out of it—in which the human figure is part and parcel of its surroundings. No horizon bounds the sea and its waves; it lies beneath a wide and limitless sky which is sharply cut by vari-coloured rocks and scattered trees. The air is full of flights of many-coloured birds, and glitters with the spray of the dolphins that splash through the waves. Amid all this animal vitality we see little skiffs full of human figures in various attitudes, assembled regardless of archaic ideas of composition; some are fishing, others steering, others again are gesticulating or simply turning round. On one of the rocks a slinger, firmly braced on his muscular legs, is about to launch his shot. He is drawn on a larger scale than the other figures. A naked diver plunges from a cliff, while on the other side of it another man clambers up with the aid of his hands. The movements of the birds, whether flying or alighting on the water, are, like those of the human figures, observed with a 'photographic' sharpness and realism that has no parallel. The picture in this tomb remains unique not only in Etruscan painting in the Ionic manner but in the whole output of archaic and, *a fortiori*, classical times, when man had become the beginning and end of art instead of being, as he is in this fresco, a mere feature of the landscape. This painter is using a figurative language that derives from Ionia and he fits with ease, therefore, into the Tarquinian tradition at a time when its standards were still vital and had not declined into empty mannerism. We have now reached the final decade of the sixth century BC.

Of other tombs belonging to the same period and the same artistic climate there are some faded and fragmentary remains. The series of Tarquinian paintings inspired by Ionia has lately been enriched by the discovery of some new examples, among which the most noteworthy are in the Tomb of the Olympiads (figs 17–19) where the ravages of time have spared some valuable details of athletic contests, games and chariot-races. The painter was less concerned with effects of colour than with design and with rendering the tense movements of the athletes; and he managed to make the chariot-race a dramatic scene both in the sense of competition he conveys and, above all, in the disaster which strikes one of the two contenders. Movement is shown not only by the gesticulations of the figures but also by the sharp lines that mark the play of muscles. The sequence of the chariot-race derives its psychological drama from the tension between the leading charioteers, and the excitement increases until it explodes with the chariot overturning amid the almost 'baroque' contortions of the horses, while the driver hurtles through the air like a disjointed puppet. Here again one should note the Etruscan character of the figure-drawing. Small details and minor narrative points are enough to invest the figures with real life: observe, for example, the way the wind created by the race blows wisps of hair across the foreheads from behind and raises a flutter of *chitons* (short tunics). The reappearance of the *phersu* episode reaffirms the Etruscan character of this painting and the Hellenic name of 'Olympiads' is extremely inappropriate to it.

It is, however, to a hand more talented in line than in colour that we must attribute the painting—small and ill-preserved—in the Tomb of the Bacchants (fig 20) at Tarquinia. The large and wide-spaced figures are separated by small trees and are shown in violent movement—which is why this tomb was incorrectly named when it was discovered. From the antiquarian's point of view the man playing the inverted lyre is interesting; but the most vivid and successful group, in its contrasts between the participants, is the one which shows a bearded man, ruddy-faced and massive, clasping a tiny girl, the elegance of whose figure is enhanced by the great *tutulus* in which her tresses are bound.

It is the Tomb of the Baron (figs 21–24) which is usually cited as the culminating point in the development of Tarquinian painting; here we are in the presence of an artistic temperament that differs from those shown in the other painted tombs. In a certain sense it was an artist of a more classic kind, a sober decorator, who composed these harmonious figures, delicate yet monumental, in a rhythm marked by the young trees that separate them. The three main figures (fig 22) in the centre of the end-wall are so placed as to suggest that they are performing ritual acts. The bearded man who, leaning on the small flautist, moves in time with the music and proffers a broad *kylix* (or shallow wine-cup) is no less restrained than the cloaked female figure facing him who raises her arms in an almost liturgical salute. Two horsemen flank the central group in a design that is mirrored with very slight variations; but with well-calculated skill the artist has changed the colour of the horses' coats and balanced the decorative effect by alternating the colours of the riders' clothing. The rhythm of the end-wall is continued on the side-walls without much alteration: on the left (fig 23) a young man stands on each side of a female figure which is cloaked like the one on the end-wall; but on the right (fig 24) the female figure is missing, while the young men, holding wreaths in their hands, make gestures of a more eloquent kind. At each side of the central group is a horseman: the two are symmetrically arranged, but their hair is differently coloured. On both sides of the false corbel that 'supports' the central roof-beam (indicated by a red stripe) the pediment contains symmetrically disposed sea-horses which uncoil their sinuous bodies amid splashing dolphins. The warm and glowing colours – red, black, violet, green and grey (originally white)—are set off by the pallor of the narrow strip that borders the frieze, and are surrounded by a greyish shadow that encloses each particular motif. The latter is a sort of priming that was applied to the rubbed-down rock where it was to be drawn or painted on. We have here either a device of style or, as I rather think, an unsuccessful technical experiment; but there is no doubt that this greyish shadow around the silhouettes increases the charm of these paintings, just as patina enhances bronze. This technical peculiarity, the remoteness of the painter's outlook from the local artistic climate of his time, the calmness of the composition, its affinities of type and style with certain groups of red-figure Attic pottery—all these, together with some other less conclusive evidence, have given ground for thinking that this is the work of a Greek. But the idea is unlikely, for this frieze shows no strong contrast with what we know of

Etruscan funerary painting either in the general scheme of its composition or in its realism, its antiquarian details, or its subject. The fact that it has been attributed to a Greek, however, serves to underline the peculiar position which the Tomb of the Baron holds among the paintings of Tarquinia in the last thirty years of the sixth century BC.

Attic Influence

Other tombs of about the same age are known at Tarquinia. Their paintings, unhappily, are ill-preserved; but one need not know most of them in order to have a true conspectus of Etruscan painting at the end of the sixth and the beginning of the fifth centuries BC. Much more serious, however, is the impossibility of satisfactorily explaining the complex decoration of later date which was recently saved from complete destruction by its removal from the Stackelberg Tomb (or Tomb of the Chariots) and transference to canvas. What we know of these paintings comes less from the photographs now available than from drawings made at the time of their discovery, or from later water-colours. Here for the first time, so far as we know, the decoration is divided into two superimposed friezes that differ in spirit and technique, although there seems no case for ascribing them to different hands. In the lower frieze the ground upon which the figures are painted is red; scenes of banqueting, dancing and music are arranged upon the end-wall and side-walls respectively, and the sections of the procession are divided by branches. The upper frieze is narrower; it has the traditional light-toned ground, and it is painted with scenes of games. This juxtaposition of friezes on different-coloured grounds has been related by some authorities—though wrongly, I believe—to Attic pottery decorated in mixed techniques, *i.e.* vases of the kind on which there are friezes of figures in both red and in black. There is nothing really new, however, about the frieze whose drawing has been compared with that of the red-figure vases (then newly invented by their potters); its language is traditionalist, indeed stereotyped, as regards the major figures, which are now mannerist in style.

It is in the upper frieze, small and lively, that we detect something really new—something that gives the paintings from the Tomb of the Chariots a supreme position in the history of Etruscan art. The figures are numerous and are arranged without that Attic *taxis* (or composition) to which we drew attention in the Tomb of the Baron; the little figures are lively and, true to the Etruscan temperament, are caught, with sharp observation, in 'characteristic' poses. Even in the preparatory drawing—the removal of the paintings has enabled their technique to be studied—their anatomy, their bodily structure and their movements have all been observed, studied and recorded with an extreme economy that extends, and certainly not by chance, to the colouring. In these figures of athletes it is easy to perceive links with red-figure vase-painting—links, indeed, with the Greek world in general which, at this very time, was passing through the stages between the late archaic and the severe that were to lead to the formulation of the canon. The artist managed to assimilate the inspiration of important Attic models (remember the quantities of Attic pottery that have been found in Etruria) without, however, deserting the traditional Etruscan spirit he had inherited. And they have indeed been fully absorbed into the Etruscan mentality, these lively compositions of people assembled on a dais to watch athletic games. In the corners formed by the side-walls with the end-wall, pieces of rudimentary architecture are drawn and they serve the additional purpose of breaking up the lengthy frieze. Part of the frieze is also devoted to the preparations for the chariot-race which gives the tomb its name and they show the successive stages by which the chariots were got ready. The design on the pediment is stylistically related to the lesser frieze, and is also novel: it shows two male figures flanking a large *krater*.

In the Tomb of the Baron (dated about 510 BC) and the Tomb of the Chariots (about 490 BC) we have two examples of high aesthetic quality from a critical period in the development not only of Etruscan painting but of Etruscan art in general. At the end of the sixth century there was a transition from the Ionic manner to the severe style. In Greece, the transition from the archaic to the severe style led on to the classical through a series of intrinsically happy experiments. These are known to us from sculpture and especially from vase-painting belonging to the first phase of red-figure technique, in which as time goes on we can see new advances being achieved in drawing and design. Foreshortening makes its appearance: the anatomical structure of the human body is rendered less and less by lines that follow convention; movements and poses are ever more closely studied in their effect on the appearance of individual limbs, muscular masses and drapery.

The Waning of Greek Influence

In Etruria, too, we find echoes of these new influences; but precisely at this crucial moment Etruria, for reasons that included politics, ceased to form part of the same system as the old, archaic Mediterranean world. She was now to find herself on the periphery of a world which perhaps she never quite understood. There was a loosening of her ties with a Greek world that was becoming classical; and Etruscan figurative art stagnates amid post-archaic stylistic formulae which it tries to refurbish without much injection of new prototypes from Greece. Yet for several decades after the beginning of the fifth century BC the influx of new Greek ideas is still perceptible in painting. Links with such groups of Attic pottery-painters as those of Kleophrades, Douris and Makron seem to have been very close. Such, indeed, was the prestige of the severe style, which was transmitted chiefly by these vase-paintings, that its ascendancy was maintained (though turned into formulae) in a local tradition or 'manner' throughout the fifth century BC.

One eloquent example of the way in which the local artisan reacted to the growth of these tendencies in Etruria during the first decades is furnished by the paintings in the Tomb of the Leopards at Tarquinia, although they must be ascribed to an artist of the second class (figs 25–27). They show no technical innovation: the colours, devoid of half-tones, are applied within irregular outlines that waver even though the stylus-marks of the preparatory drawing are still quite visible. But certain antiquarian details (such as the fact that the Ionic *tutulus* was no longer in fashion with women) and certain stylistic advances (in more than one case the eye is shown almost in profile) suggest a later period than the one to which the Tomb of the Chariots is assigned. On the end-wall, below the two spotted feline beasts that have given the tomb its name, a banqueting-scene is painted; on elaborate triple couches six wreathed figures recline, two of them being fair-haired ladies, while two servants, one with a pitcher and the other with a sieve, stand erect between the *klinai* (fig 26). On the side walls, subdivided by the usual trees, appears a procession consisting of dancers (fig 25) and musicians (fig 27). Notwithstanding the impression of lively colour which it makes at first sight—partly because the paintings are well-preserved—the Tomb of the Leopards is heavy and rather vulgar and must be classed as old-fashioned in comparison with others of the same artistic period which, moreover, handle very much the same subjects.

What is usually considered the masterpiece of the Tarquinian school of this period—though it is actually slightly later (about 470 BC)—is the decoration of the Tomb of the Triclinium which was rescued a few years ago and removed. The name shows at once that its subject is the same as that of the Tomb of the Leopards and there is a similar arrangement of the friezes in both. But what an artistic difference they show! The principal scene, that on the end-wall, is seriously damaged and indeed on the left there remains nothing at all of one of the *klinai*. Here again there are servants with the guests, while tame domestic animals at the foot of the couches lend interest to the scene. The composition is static, but relieved by variations in the poses, by the gestures of the arms and by the inclinations of the heads. Better preserved are the paintings of dances on the side-walls. Here again, dancers and musicians are separated by little trees; but in the Tomb of the Triclinium the artist has applied a fresh imagination to this traditional feature. He has varied the spaces between the trees and painted little animals and birds beneath them. Two groups of dancers in which youths and maidens alternate (see, for example, figs 28 and 29) set out in the footsteps of a flautist (fig 30) and, on the opposite wall (fig 31), of a lyre-player. The figures are infused with a sense of fluid and harmonious vigour which rises at times to ecstatic abandon. The rhythm that links them is developed in a play of curves that echo from end to end of the wall and are reinforced by a balanced counterpoint of colour-areas and of repetitions in the pattern of draperies. The painter of this tomb is one of the major figures not only in Etruscan painting but in Etruscan art. His aesthetic sense was highly refined; he was no improviser but a practised hand (no signs of preparatory drawing are visible), firm in execution and sapient in the orchestration of colour.

There is another tomb at Tarquinia, of slightly later date (about 460 BC), the Tomb of the Funeral Couch. Despite much damage, it displays a quality little inferior to that of the Tomb of the Triclinium with which, indeed, it shows stylistic and technical analogies. One may not agree with some authorities who see the same painter's hand in both tombs, but one can nevertheless assert that the painter of the Tomb of the Funeral Couch profited by the work of the earlier master. The name of this tomb is derived from a great catafalque with two striped or wreathed cones placed on cushions, which is shown under a canopy upheld by two small leaf-hung poles. The pedimental triangle has been subtracted from the end-wall on which this is painted and added to the area of the upper frieze. The scenes with figures are placed on either side of the catafalque: to the right, on two levels (a feature in which some have seen reflected the inventions of Polygnotus of Thasos) the banqueters appear; on the left, however, nothing remains but a female figure. There is little doubt that we have here a ritual scene, and it very likely represents a stage in the rites of the dead. On the side-walls there are groups of musicians, female dancers, athletes and figures playing various games. Among the details, the group of young men with the horse (fig 32) has become famous for the harmony of its composition and the fluency of its drawing. The fact that the blue of the horse's coat is 'untrue' and conventional does not diminish the sense of real life which the group conveys.

These are works of high artistic quality; but there are other tombs at Tarquinia which show that even minor painters were open to the ideas and formulae of the severe style. Among them were those (around the middle of the fifth century BC) who decorated the tomb called after Francesca Giustiniani, the Tomb of the Maiden and the Querciola Tomb (otherwise called the Tomb of the Boar Hunt).

Typical of the first and best-preserved of these (figs 43–45) are figures of unusual size. The design, however, is flat; and the limitations of the painter's vision are not concealed by the variety of the poses, nor by the richness of the details that are mechanically distributed over the clothing. The colour, however, makes a generally vivid effect. Some of the motifs, too, are still aesthetically effective—for example, the pair of horses: there is a striking contrast of colour between the war-horse in the foreground and its blue-coated mate. If we accept the explanation put forward by some students, this is the first time in Etruscan painting that we find the journey to the Beyond being performed by coach.

The presence of very second-rate works in this group may perhaps betray a decline in the quality of the painters at Tarquinia. In that case, the drying-up of artistic springs, combined with an economic crisis in the Etruscan world, would explain why painted tombs henceforth become scarce. At Tarquinia, so far as we can judge from what has been discovered, they are missing altogether for a long period—from the end of the fifth century until well into the fourth.

From the first decades of the fifth century BC we possess pictorial records at other Etruscan centres: Veii and Clusium.

Among the painted terracotta plaques at Veii, amid the ruins of a sacred edifice at Portonaccio, a fragment of great interest came to light (fig 33). It shows a woman's head, seen full-face, slightly inclined; her right hand, which has survived, holds her orange-red hair and the same pigment has been used to heighten her cheeks. Elsewhere, colours have been applied with faint brush-strokes. This lovely fragment can be dated about 480 BC.

There were several examples of funerary painting of the fifth century at Clusium, but the best-preserved belong to the first half. Of others we have only copies and in most cases it is very difficult to study their style so as to arrange them in date order.

The most complete set is in the Tomb of the Monkey which consists of a central chamber that opens into three others. The lower frieze runs around the walls of the principal chamber, interrupted by the door-openings, and it shows athletic games and displays of skill. The tomb received its name on account of a little monkey in a tree next to a group of two wrestlers who are watched by an umpire; nearby, a young man is displaying skill in horsemanship with two horses (fig. 34). Elsewhere, we find other athletes: a javelin-thrower, boxers (fig 35), etc. The chief personage (perhaps the owner of the tomb) is a female figure who watches the spectacle from under an umbrella. Before her, to the music of a flautist wearing a strange headpiece, a girl is dancing with a sort of candelabrum balanced on her head. The same subject, with slight variations due to its different date and location, was found recently at Tarquinia, on the walls of the tomb called the Tomb of the Jugglers. Its iconographic analogy with the smaller frieze in the Tomb of the Chariots is obvious, but this tomb at Clusium is later (about 470 BC). Points to note are the great size of the heads, the difference of scale among the figures in a single section of the frieze, and the ingenuousness of many details. This provincialism is typical of the art of Clusium in general, for it remained behindhand in comparison with that of other centres closer to the sea. Clusium showed greater uniformity and in a sense a more native character even when it applied advances made elsewhere; it simply adapted them without having felt them deeply or re-lived them for itself.

The paintings from the Tomb of the Colle Casuccini were removed in 1953, but they were badly damaged and had been seriously spoiled by nineteenth-century restorations. The subjects of the frieze are the usual ones: banquets, athletic games, dances and chariot-races (figs 36–42). Their artistic range is no wider than that of the Tomb of the Monkey, even though they belong to a later period. The drawing, so far as the restoration leaves it visible, is weak; it is chiefly the colouring that confers a certain decorative effect. But the painters of this tomb achieved no unity of style. As was the case in the Tomb of the Monkey, they made use, albeit rather mechanically, of the inherited stock of types; but in justice it must be said that here and there in this tomb they achieved a fairly unified composition, not only through the harmonious distribution of their colours but also in the drawing of the outlines. In this frieze, at any rate, there are none of those disparities in the size of the figures in a single section of the frieze that we noted in the Tomb of the Monkey; the stock-types are here adjusted to the height available.

From the Archaic to the Hellenistic Period

Between the archaic group of Etruscan tomb-paintings and the one which, starting in the last decades of the fourth century BC, is usually called Hellenistic, there is not only a long gap in the series of examples but also a profound change in spiritual content, and thus in the range of subjects. The Beyond is compounded of ingredients from Greek mythology but is transposed into an atmosphere of terror-filled nightmare. It appears upon the walls of the tombs in scenes that combine Hellenic elements with typically native monsters and demons. If we compare the painting of the fourth century onwards with that of the first phase, therefore, we cannot fail to notice that the artists were no more than spasmodically, and in a few happy details, capable of rising above a mediocre level of style and technique.

The great Greek painting of the second half of the fifth and the fourth centuries was slow in becoming known. The spirit of classical art, as far as painting is concerned, made itself felt in rhythmic and harmonious composition and, indeed, in one exceptional piece, in iconography: this piece is the painted sarcophagus from Tarquinia (figs 46 and 47) now in the Archaeological Museum at Florence.

The four sides of this sarcophagus carry representations of fights between Greeks and Amazons—a theme that was very popular in Greek art and which was also much exploited in Hellenic painting from the time of Polygnotus of Thasos to that of Mikon. On a blue and pink background the figures are shown in lively movement, harmonised by fluency of line, and they make a vivid plastic effect that is classical in nature and owes much to the colour. Painting on a sarcophagus has, of course, characteristics and possibilities that are absent from painting on large areas of wall in the bowels of the earth; on the well-prepared stone the artist has achieved a delicacy of effect that we associate with easel-painting. The faces of the Amazons, in particular, show pathos in a way that was unthinkable before the middle of the fourth century.

Each of the short sides represents, in different forms, a Greek falling beneath the blows of the Amazons (see, for example, fig 46); one of the long sides shows a group of Amazons attacking two Greeks, while the other shows the combatants in four-horsed chariots (fig 47). This last is the finest part of the decoration, and the group of white horses bears eloquent witness to the artist's mastery in the use of line and *chiaroscuro*. Affinities have been found between this painting and the style of certain vases produced in Italy; this observation has led to the conjecture that the artist was a Greek painter from southern Italy or perhaps an Etruscan pupil who had learnt his trade well.

Also to the end of the fourth century belong the paintings from the two Golini tombs at Orvieto which, though in very bad condition, were detached and are now in the Archaeological Museum at Florence (fig 48). To judge from old drawings the frieze from the more important tomb must have been interesting, both for its subject (a banquet in the Beyond, in the presence of Hades and Persephone) and for its artistic qualities, although it appears only to be the work of a sound provincial. The classical modelling of the figures is enlivened by a very Etruscan kind of animation (a little overdone, perhaps) and by a taste for realistic detail. Other tombs in the Orvieto area (for example the Tomb of the Hescanas) are only inadequately recorded in old drawings.

Much the same subject as in the Golini tomb (the banquet in the Beyond) is found at Tarquinia in what is now called the Tomb of Orcus. Two tombs of different ages have been linked by a passage in which was painted—perhaps at a still later date—a scene showing the blinding of Polyphemus by Ulysses (fig 55). The paintings in the older tomb, which is generally considered to be of the same age as the Golini tomb, have suffered grave damage, but from the remaining fragments we can judge that they were of good quality. The subject is a banquet: of the couples stretched out on the *kline* on the right-hand wall there remains the head of Arnth Velcha's wife—a lady who henceforth figures in the anthology of ancient art (fig 50). The inscription gives us her personal name, Velia. Her face is painted in profile, but we are given a three-quarter view of what remains of her shoulders, which are clothed in a tunic and a cloak with a scalloped border. The lady is wearing her jewels—two necklaces and ear-rings with pendants; her reddish-brown hair is loose in front and falls in ringlets down the sides of her face, but on her forehead it is held by a wreath of green leaves and it is gathered on the nape of the neck in a woven *sphendoné* or sling-shaped support. The clear-cut profile is of a purity that recalls certain coins, and the eye has a melancholy look which is, in turn, reinforced by the dark line that descends from the corner of the mouth. Extreme discretion is used in the shading on the cheeks, around the nose and above the eye. To give more prominence to this noble head the artist employed a device suggested by the subject of the scene—the murk of the Beyond, which forms a dense curtain of mist behind the figures. The light-toned parts of the head coincide exactly with the height of this greenish-black zone and are shown up by it sharply; while at the exact point where the coppery hair rises from the noble brow and where the top of the *sphendoné* comes, the artist has lightened the background to show up the coiffure and the wreath. On the left-hand wall, beneath a design of hanging foliage, a monstrous figure has survived: it is Charu, livid of flesh, beaked of nose, snake-haired, with great wings and a cloak (fig 49). Before his hideous face a winged serpent uncoils itself. Here, for the first time in Etruscan painting, we come face to face with one of those monsters which, though taken from the stock of classical art, were so widely used in the art of Etruria—with the emphasis laid on those qualities of terror and repulsiveness which the Greeks did not care to see exhibited even for religious purposes.

In the later tomb the paintings represent the Beyond of the Greeks, mingled with Etruscan demonology. The place of honour is given to the lords of the underworld, Aita (Hades) and Phersipnai (Persephone)—both of them Greek in type, but with Etruscan additions such as the green snakes in the goddess's hair and the wolf-skin on the shoulders of the god. The Greek heroes who figure in Hellenic representations of the underworld are also here: Ajax, the shade of Tiresias, and Agamemnon (fig 54) near a tree in which little black figures, the souls, can be seen climbing. We see, too, the torture of Sisyphus and the gloomy prison of Pirithöus and Theseus, and, in front of the lords, Geryon (fig 51). In strident contrast with these sad and majestic figures from the Greek land of the dead is the monstrous Tuchulcha—a personage who differs little from the Charu of the first tomb, and is no less terrifying. Wings alone give a supernatural character to a young demon who, with a wingless companion (fig 52), is shown near a table with rich vases (fig 53).

This frieze in the second Tomb of Orcus can be dated about the end of the third century BC or the beginning of the second. The impression it makes is due not only to its aesthetic merit and its subject but, even more, to the great wealth of motifs which the artist has combined.

The third century BC, again, is the date of the paintings in the Tomb of the Shields at Tarquinia, with their banqueting scenes (figs 56–58). Their lay-out is complex: it includes doors and windows, and the shields which give the tomb its name are painted in a smaller side-chamber. Abundant inscriptions provide the names of the persons (members of the Velcha family) who are taking part in the banquet. The frieze, with its predominant red-brown, black and white in various shades, at once makes the impression of a careful catalogue of wealth: the clothes and the coverings of the triple couches are sumptuous; the fittings are rich, the feast is copious and enlivened with music (fig 57) and a throng of servants attends (fig 58). A tutelary spirit writes on a double tablet in silent allusion to the place where the banquet takes place—the Beyond. The owners of the tomb and their relations are shown in a manner that varies but slightly from one *kline* to another. The man is semi-recumbent and his gestures and looks show affection for his female companion. Following the new fashion, she is seated beside him on the bed. The inscriptions in this tomb, as well as the carefully distinguished individuality of the persons, make it clear that the intention was to flatter the aristocratic pride of the last descendants of the Velcha family; but the most interesting point is the attempt at genuine facial portraiture—of the men in particular. The paintings in the Tomb of the Shields thus form a group of great significance in the history of Etruscan portrait-painting. In some cases the artist has succeeded in capturing, one feels, not only the facial likeness of his sitter but also a degree of essential truth. An example is the face of Larth Velcha (fig 56), seen in three-quarter view: it is watchful and strained, like the faces one sometimes sees in early 'posed' photographs. Details are summarily drawn, from the shorthand rendering of the stubbly beard to the aristocratically curving nose. Some of the other portraits differ, however, from this one: the difference is not only in the sad expression of the sitters but also in the technical handling—full of half-tones and impressionistic in some of the details. On the grounds of these inequalities and of others in the pictorial handling, one would put this decorator down as a mediocre artist; it looks as if his attempt to render strong emotion was incompatible with the craftsman's tradition that shows in the faithful but flat transcription of figures and objects.

The François Tomb from Vulci is now in Rome, in the possession of Prince Torlonia, its painting having been almost entirely removed a century ago. This grandiose decoration was composed of scenes—gruesome and infernal, of course—from Greek mythology and scenes from local history in which the brothers Vibenna (Vipina) and Mastarna (Macstrna) appear on the one hand and Cn. Tarquinius 'romanus' on the other. There are also portraits of bygone members of the *gens* Saties, who owned the tomb. Expert opinion dates the tomb variously between the end of the fourth century and the beginning of the first century BC. At present there is a tendency to prefer the latest date, *i.e.* the beginning of the first century BC. The portraits are noteworthy: the characters are well differentiated and the expressions varied, though uniformly melancholy. The portrait of Vel Saties is considered by some perceptive authorities to be the only genuine portrait that has survived from ancient painting before the first age of imperial Rome. The historical and mythological friezes are drawn from various sources and one might well talk of eclecticism; but the decorator brought originality as well as inventiveness to his complicated task and never lost control. In the Trojan scene of the massacre of the prisoners on the tumulus of Patroclus, the demons of the Etruscan Beyond, Charu and Vanth, are once again present in order to give a local tinge to a scene that derives, no doubt, from some Greek composition. But by now, Etruscan figurative art had taken this scene over from the Greek world, as it did so many scenes of murder and bloodshed that are repeated in abundance on sarcophagi and urns belonging to the last phase of Etruscan civilisation. And in the François Tomb we once more find the group of Eteocles and Polynices; other episodes, however, such as that of Ajax and Cassandra, are rare in Etruscan art. In these paintings, too, there is a new hint at the Beyond in the torture of Sisyphus: but the presence of Phoenix and Nestor (fig 59) has no clear significance. Their figures are not shown enacting a scene but in a kind of 'portrait' at the sides of a door; and their positions correspond to those of two Etruscan personages, Vel Saties and a lady who appear on the opposite wall.

Asiatic Hellenism

The series of Etruscan funerary paintings ends with the Tomb of the Typhon at Tarquinia—a large sepulchre in which, however, the painted frieze is confined to the four-sided central column and to a short length of the right-hand wall. The sides of the column facing the left- and right-hand walls are painted with two winged giants whose legs end in snakes. The better-preserved is the one on the right (fig 60). This mighty apparition advances in bold perspective and is tense with strain, for in fact the Typhon is shown supporting the roof of the tomb with his hands. The head, seen in full-face, is damaged; but the great staring eyes, deep-sunk beneath the arching, rugged brow, recall the Hellenistic giants of the type best seen in the Pergamum frieze. The tangled hair is coloured blue like the snaked ends of the legs and like the great arms with their modelling in light and shade. By this architectonic and ornamental device of the giant, Etruscan painting, along with numerous examples of sculpture, bears witness to the influx of Asiatic Hellenism. The scene on the right-hand wall is sadly damaged but still interesting. It remains within the Etruscan tradition in its final phase, being shot through with horror in the face of death. A group of white-robed persons are driven forward by demons with torches and hammers. There is much variety in the treatment of the figures, in the placing and the view of their faces, with their intensity of expression and their individual characterisation. The heads are drawn on different planes, partially overlapping, and the folds of the draperies blend together. All these features form part of the Roman manner as we see it in realistic and historical bas-reliefs. Yet the painting belongs to the fourth century BC.

Southern Italian Tomb Painting

In southern Italy, too, the practice of painting tombs—whether rock-cut or, more often, built of blocks of stone—was fairly widespread. Few tombs of this type have yet been discovered, however, although there have been some recent finds. A large part of the southern Italian funerary paintings known to us is now lost, and for these one must rely on old drawings that are not always faithful. The majority of interrelated examples come from a period in which southern Italy was already Hellenised but was also in constant contact with the non-Greek people of the interior, and when prosperous centres arose where pottery was made and painted in the Attic tradition. In this pottery, nevertheless, we can to some extent detect features that must be ascribed to the 'barbarian' element of the South. We must take the pottery of Campania and Paestum into account in addition to the two Italiot traditions, the Apulian and the Lucanian, when considering the funerary painting of this region. These examples of vase-painting are interesting but not of high quality. Only a handful of specialists have hitherto studied them and one can make only this general mention of them here.

The centres in which painted tombs have been found are in Campania (at Cumae, Nola and especially at Capua), in Lucania (at Paestum and its neighbourhood), in Samnium (at Allifae) and in the Apulian country (Ruvo and Gnathia). As a whole, these tombs can be assigned to a fairly long period stretching from the first quarter of the fifth century BC to the beginning of the second century; but the most impressive group belongs to the fourth century.

In these funerary paintings, as well as in most of the Etruscan ones, the porous rock was surfaced with plaster and the decorator then divided the wall into three strips. Between the dado and an upper band ran the main frieze. Their themes are various: games, ladies dressing their hair, the departure, or more often the return, of warriors, victorious or wounded, and scenes of bloody battles. Despite a resemblance to more or less contemporary Etruscan tomb-paintings, the spirit revealed by the friezes in the southern Italian tombs is different: so are their style and their artistic level.

Perhaps the most interesting of the tomb-paintings of southern Italy are, alas, lost; and it is difficult indeed to accept water-colour drawings made by people with very varied training and artistic attainments as substitutes. All one can give here is a selection of the most noteworthy examples that have been brought from various places (Cumae, Ruvo, and Paestum) and are now in the National Museum at Naples (figs 61–64).

Of interest to the antiquarian is the representation of a lady dressing, which comes from a tomb at Cumae (fig 61). From the point of view of style, we see native features side by side with Greek, not only in details of costume but also in the rustic look which strikes the most casual observer. This painting belongs to the second half of the fourth century BC. A good deal more vivid is the frieze (a detail from it is given in fig 62) from a tomb at Ruvo whose date, however, is a century earlier. It shows a number of women dancing: they form a long, tight chain and they are swathed in heavy draperies that leave only their arms and faces visible. This is a work of high aesthetic interest that deserves to figure in any selection of ancient painting. There is no doubt that it represents a funeral rite—a kind of mourning chant. It is an old traditional rite, however, and has lost all genuine emotion. Its continued performance is more a piece of folk-lore, and only the austere garments suggest the idea of death. Indeed, the theme would be monotonous if the artist had not varied it by introducing a few figures which interrupt the rhythm of the lamentations and, especially, by using variations of colour in the garments and in their details.

About a century later than this tomb is one at Paestum (figs 63 and 64 give some details) which is, however, a little stereotyped, especially in the pains with which robust anatomy and details of costume are rendered. The figures here are well spaced out in a kind of procession to which the neutral background gives a certain triumphal majesty. The subject is the return of the men from a battle in which, while suffering losses, they have captured some trophies from their enemies. The lamentations are infused with a spirit of martial rhetoric that recalls the spirit of the 'popular' pictures which used to be carried aloft in the processions at triumphs in Rome and which displayed appropriate episodes of the campaign just concluded.

It is still difficult to reach full understanding of the subjects that are found in the funerary painting of continental southern Italy. The allusions to death, when explicit, show us a conception of the Beyond very different from what we can deduce from contemporary Etruscan work. Apart from the funeral dance represented at Ruvo, death is often alluded to by means of symbols such as the pomegranate and the egg. In the scenes of duels and of returns from war the fame gained by the family on the field of battle takes priority; death is only indirectly present.

A mere episode, provincial, marginal, limited, and lacking in further development—such is the brief, inconclusive story of ancient painting in the decoration of aristocratic tombs in the extreme south of the Italian peninsula. Yet, if it would be wrong to ignore Italiot pottery, it would be no less unjust to omit all mention of these tombs from a discussion of ancient painting in the peninsula.

Roman Painting

Native and Greek Influences

Roman pictorial art, whether republican or imperial, is hardly mentioned in ancient literature; no individual artist seems to have become famous, nor did any work of art become popular or celebrated as so many Greek paintings did in the fourth century BC or in Hellenistic times. Painting, in fact, was left to slaves or freedmen, or to the occasional plebeian; and Romans who painted were remembered only as curiosities. The figurative arts in general were regarded in Rome as marginal activities, and this again is a cause of the anonymity in which the history of Roman painting is wrapped. Signatures, too, are rare and appear only on works of little importance; most of them, moreover, are Greek. We know that among the oldest specimens of Roman painting were the triumphal pictures; but doubt may be felt about their artistic value. Whether displayed in the temples or carried in the triumphal processions, their quality can hardly have been much different from that of the popular *ex voto* pictures or the narrative placards which the professional story-tellers use, in countries where illiteracy is common, when recounting current events or folk-tales. We possess no Roman funerary painting of great antiquity; but a fragment from a tomb on the Esquiline, with narrative pictures placed one above the other, points to the existence of memorial tomb-painting in later times (third and second centuries BC). Painted *imagines maiorum* (ancestral portraits) must also have been common in aristocratic families and such portraits were doubtless of a less 'popular' kind—perhaps resembling the ones of which we have examples in later Etruscan funerary painting. By their very nature, of course, the votive pictures carried in processions, like the topical pictures—almost posters—of gladiatorial contests, must have aimed at achieving a wide popular appeal.

In contrast with these 'native' productions we have examples of another pictorial tradition—cultivated, Greek in origin or execution, or Greek at least in inspiration. As a result of the Roman expansion into Magna Graecia and later into the Greek world in Asia, works of art flowed into Rome, and paintings occupy no minor place in the accounts given by historians. To a large extent they were the spoils of war or were acquired by generals and officials. A frenzy of collecting then began and in many cases was pursued to excess—especially in the late republican period and in early imperial times. But along with Greek works of art (a large proportion of which were used for the decoration of public places), Rome and the other chief cities of the Roman state saw the arrival of Greek artists. Some came as slaves; others, of their own free choice.

The elder Pliny summed up the difference between classical Greek and Roman painting by remarking that Greek painting was done on *tabulae* (*i.e.* it was easel-painting), whereas Roman painting was done on walls. We need not concern ourselves with the social and moral considerations which Pliny deduced from this observation; but his remark itself is not devoid of truth. For the Romans, painting was employed as an ornament to architecture; it was decorative mural painting, whose proper subjects were architecture or landscapes. Ludius (or Studius) is supposed, according to Pliny, to have been the first to paint landscapes on the walls of houses.

The Four Pompeian Styles

Of decorative mural painting in the Roman world of about the second century BC until the eighth decade AD we have abundant examples in Pompeian painting. (We shall use the adjective 'Pompeian'—now generic—to denote the objects discovered in the city and the villas buried by the eruption of Vesuvius in AD 79.) This mural painting was governed by certain decorative norms derived from the architectonic properties of the walls for which it was destined. Every single mural painting bears witness to the decorator's struggle with the monumental nature of the wall, which therefore had to be reduced, split up or spaced out by means of *trompe l'oeil* architectural perspectives, gardens (figs 67–69), panels containing reproductions of other paintings (fig 66), figures and motifs detached from their background. As long ago as the nineteenth century Professor Mau propounded a classification of the rules that governed the decoration of a given space; and his study was so thorough that the four 'Pompeian styles' are spoken of even today, as though Pompeii had been the headquarters of Roman decorative painting in the last centuries BC and the first century AD. Mau's classifications are still followed in their general lines, although more than one amendment has been made to them and they have been worked out in greater detail. The first 'style' is that of 'facing with marble': that is to say, the wall was painted to look as though it were faced with rectangular blocks of marble—usually polychrome. In addition to sculptural or pictorial friezes inset in the wall, we find architectonic features realistically painted and fully justified by their allusion to architectural elements within the mural paintings. This type of decoration originated in the Hellenistic world and goes back at least to the second century BC. In the second 'style' the architectonic features of the wall are emphasized; the wall is illusionistically moved back by inserting architectural features in the foreground, and the scene represented lies behind them. This method of mural decoration was introduced in Rome in the second century BC and its origin also lies somewhere in the Asiatic part of the Hellenistic world. It is on this kind of wall that the great cycles were painted: the one in the Villa of the Mysteries outside Pompeii (figs 70–75) and the one in the Villa at Boscoreale (figs 76–79) to which we shall be referring later. In the fourth 'style' we discern four phases today; they did not follow one another chronologically, however, but more or less coexisted. There are examples in which, amid articulated buildings with projecting wings, we find clear signs of the division of the wall-space into aedicules, as well as architectural perspectives against landscape-backgrounds; or again, once the point has been reached where the wall is frankly subdivided, the scheme is expanded *ad libitum* into large compositions of architectural perspectives on more than one plane. The room is illusionistically enlarged beyond the walls; and in the final phase the walls themselves are abolished, to reveal a fugue of architectural fantasies. The fourth 'style', in fact, is only a further phase of the second; and in Pompeii it ended only with the death of the city. If the second 'style' with its final phase lasted into the later years of Augustus, the beginnings of the fourth can be assigned to the time of his Julian and Claudian successors. Walls are loaded with a superabundance of fantastic and irrational painted architecture, with perspectives seen through windows and doors, with imitation polychrome marble, with swags and sumptuous superstructures. The third 'style', on the other hand, (roughly contemporaneous with the final phase of the second) is no longer based upon architectural scene-painting but on a division of the wall into monochrome panels with precise and almost linear decoration, with fantastic juxtapositions, Vestal features, stylised or realistic, human figures, animals, and delicate architectural motifs. These are the purely ornamental decorations which enjoyed so remarkable a vogue from the Renaissance onwards under the name of 'grotesques'. Real pictures were inserted in these frames—being often copies of works which enjoyed great renown (like most of those illustrated here) or scenes and figures floating, as it were, in space against backgrounds of red, black, yellow or green.

The foregoing scheme of classification should not be taken as rigid; moreover it does not cover all the examples that have been found (their variety greatly exceeds the available categories) in the houses of the Vesuvian cities and contemporary houses elsewhere. Examples of post-

Flavian Roman painting are available only in very broken series and in fragments that are far from numerous. If the truth be told, such painting is largely unknown, although efforts have been made to reconstruct the history of its development after the disaster at Pompeii; but these efforts have either been frustrated by the many gaps or have erred on the side of excessive schematisation.

Undue prominence in the history of Roman painting has been given by the hand of chance to the phase which coincides with the final centuries in the life of the Vesuvian cities. It must be pointed out, too, that the bulk of Pompeian wall-paintings date from after the earthquake of AD 62 or 63. Our examples therefore are unevenly distributed. Yet Pompeii was only a provincial city and most of its inhabitants were people of no great refinement: with a few exceptions their craftsmen were modestly gifted. Just as in our own times, some craftsmen held to tradition while others, reluctant to be out of date, tried their best to keep up—to follow the fashions which Vitruvius so severely criticised for displaying that luxury to which the elder Pliny had attributed the decay of Roman standards. Greater refinement is suggested by Herculaneum and also Stabiae—places which, like the suburban villas of Pompeii, have yielded paintings of as good a quality as has been found in Pompeian houses of the most luxurious kind.

Sources of Pompeian 'Pictures'

If countless arguments—many still in progress—have been caused by Roman mural painting as a whole, more dissension still has been provoked by the 'pictures' and the friezes that are scattered among the architectonic features, especially in the third and fourth 'styles'. These are above all pictures of mythological subjects derived from Greece (illustrations of Roman myths are very rare indeed) and the models from which they derive are also for the most part plainly Greek. Nevertheless one must in general accept the name of 'Romano-Hellenistic' painting which has been given to the 'Pompeian' pictures and to their Roman contemporaries.

What are the origins of these pictures? Many paintings from the Vesuvian cities, Rome, and other places repeat the same subject (see, for example, two versions of the same picture in figs 94 and 96, and figs 95 and 97): neither the variations nor the additions, the compressions, the inversions of the figures, nor even the differences in the execution, suffice to conceal their fundamental identity. As a result it has been conjectured that the painters—mere craftsmen who were making pictures of the same subject—had a common archetype, to be sought among major paintings. In some cases indeed it is reasonable to think that the model which the copyists had before them was derived not from a picture but from some piece of sculpture—for example, the Centaur and Achilles in fig 80 (according to Pliny there was a famous group of Chiron and Achilles, by an unknown sculptor, set up in the Saepta Julia in Rome) or the Three Graces (fig 111); and derivation from sculpture is easy to detect in many of the figures in scenes and friezes. We are faced, therefore, with the work of copyists who worked not always from originals but also from notebooks or collections of stray sketches, or from 'atlases' that were widely known and copied for themselves. Sometimes they translated their material into a different formal language, at other times they varied it within the limits dictated by the master-theme, and in certain cases they actually painted creatively—though they never abandoned the Hellenistic manner that was now their natural mode of expression. These observations apply to almost the whole of 'Pompeian' picture-painting. The sources of these pictures have also been sought; and the picture of Hercules and the infant Telephus (fig 86), for example, has been linked with the art of Pergamum precisely because of the link between that city and this rarely encountered myth. It is the subject, again, which suggests a link between Alexandrian art and the picture of the arrival of Io in Egypt (fig 106), while a link with the Nile Delta can be seen in the style and content of the highly Egyptian religious ceremony in fig 113.

In a few cases the originals of many pictures can be attributed to painters whose names appear in ancient literature. For the original of the crudely painted picture shown in fig 87 the name of Timanthes has been suggested—a painter who, finding himself unable to impart a proper degree of suffering to the face of Agamemnon in a scene of the sacrifice of Iphigenia, gave her father a veil. The Medea by Timomachus was very famous in antiquity and there is an echo of it to be found in the Medea at Herculaneum (fig 88)—a figure which is superb in its pose and plastic rendering. In the picture reproduced in fig 89, the scheme has been changed by heightening the colour-contrasts of the garments while exploiting the pattern of detail in the background—but the pathos has vanished. To give an example from mosaics, there is no doubt that some painting of the end of the fourth century BC or of the early Hellenistic age is the source of the mosaic of the Battle of Issus (see fig 143 for a detail)—a painting for which various artists have been suggested: Aristides of Thebes, Philoxenos of Eretria and Helena, the daughter of Timon the Egyptian. To the credit for the mosaic of the doves on the basin (of which we have an enlarged copy from Pompeii—see fig 168), Sosos, who was suggested by Pliny, has a better claim than Pliny's words convey.

Wall-paintings with life-sized figures are also copies (with variations of style and arrangement which cannot always be established) of Hellenistic originals that are either lost or not mentioned in documents. The 'historical' frieze from the Villa at Boscoreale (now, alas, split up among several museums) derives from an early Hellenistic painting, and the fragment now in the Naples Museum (figs 76–79), as generally interpreted, represents figures at the court of Antigonus II of Macedonia. The bodies are massive and the draperies exuberant. Colour predominates: here and there it is handled impressionistically, and line is lost amid the baroque convolutions of the draperies. One can date the copy to the middle of the second century AD.

The large frieze of the Villa of the Mysteries (figs 70–75) offers another case in which the painter was inspired by some composition by a great master; but he transposed it into a language of his own—one that shows high technical skill (with some obvious weaknesses: for example, certain clumsy foreshortenings and the handling of the draperies) though lyrical ardour is not its strongest point. Its archetype has been dated anywhere from the fifth to the first centuries BC; but the frieze of the Villa of the Mysteries is generally thought to have been painted around the middle of the first century, *i.e.* a little before the Boscoreale one. Colour is subordinate to line; the modelling is vigorous but does not disturb the unity of the grandiose composition. The whole frieze is constructed around an ideal centre which is occupied by the figures of Dionysus and Ariadne—the latter ,unhappily, being damaged (fig 74). To the left is a quiet, slow-moving scene (figs 70–72) which culminates in the idyllic episode of the daughter of Pan suckling a kid (fig 73). The calm is violently interrupted by a female figure in rapid movement (fig 73 again) but is agreeably restored by the group of Silenus and the satyrs (fig 74, left). To the right of Dionysus and Ariadne a dramatic movement begins with the unveiling of the fertility-symbol, or *phallus*; it passes to the winged female with the whip and thence to the girl who is about to undergo flagellation and she is followed, as if in a sudden *allegro*, by the nude female dancer (fig 75). Various learned interpretations have been advanced, but no agreement has yet been reached; all that is certain is that we have here a religious scene, connected with Dionysus, in which women are taking an active part.

In the large pictures that occupy the central section of the walls it is mythological subjects that predominate: with heroes and heroines in episodes and situations we can often recognise from literature (such as the episodes from the *Iliad* of which good examples are given in figs 90 91 and 92), or from the great Attic tragedies of the fifth century BC (for examples see figs 87, 88, 89, 98, 101). But in many cases these stories have lost much of their majestic grandeur—a grandeur which archaic and classical Greek art had successfully (if sometimes ingenuously) maintained but which now reaches us through the filter of that Hellenistic spirit so evident in literature. Other paintings also are fully Hellenistic from this point of view; and that subtle eroticism we know so well from Hellenistic poetry is at the source of paintings in which gods and heroes (Mars in fig 104, Hercules in fig 108—and there are plenty more) are caught in the toils of love and are conquered by feminine beauty. Little cupids are one of the commonest features in paintings of the period and appear with great frequency also in its decorative art; they are brought in not only to create an atmosphere but sometimes as protagonists too. There is no illustration here of the well-known scenes from the small frieze in the House of the Vettii, nor of others in the same taste. Among the larger paintings, too, (of which it seems enough to give an example in fig 109, with a detail in fig 110) there are many in which the erotic features are introduced by way of flavouring, to give the subject a particular relish.

The myth itself is an elegiac conception which not infrequently turns into *genre*, and is now no longer taken from Homer but from Apollonius Rhodius, Callimachus, Theocritus or one of the many other Hellenistic poets. Painting and poetry developed along similar lines and reached the same form of expression. One of the most popular themes is Dionysus with his licentious crew; and such themes are treated sometimes from the sensual angle, sometimes from the sentimental, sometimes again more intimately as, for example, in the painting illustrated in fig 107 (the ugly figure of Hermes on the right, clumsy and out of proportion, was added by the copyist), where the well-known scene becomes a lively little *genre* picture of country life. Apart from their spirit, the pictures themselves transport us, by their choice of subject, to the world we know from Hellenistic literature. Their delicate pictorial visions of landscape may be a mere setting, subordinate to the story (*e.g.* figs 103, 107, 109— though in most cases one wonders if the story was not added by the copyist), or they may be the true subject of the picture, in which case the human figures are mere accessories, equal in value to the rocks, the country shrines, the flocks or the stunted trees (*e.g.* figs 118 and 119). These landscapes are idyllic, imaginary, peaceful and happy. To Ludius (or Studius), the painter of the Augustan age already mentioned, it is usual to attribute not only the invention of landscape in general but, even more, the large-scale introduction of views of villas with porticoes, of seaside towns, and of ports—a class of painting which, if it did not originate in Rome, certainly enjoyed the widest popularity in Roman decorative art (see figs 120 and 121). In addition to the bucolic and architectonic types of landscape, there are paintings of gardens that cover entire walls—such as those in Livia's Roman villa at Prima Porta (figs 67–69) and others at Pompeii—gardens enlivened with flowers, birds, hedges and trellises, and full of atmosphere, with the plants clearly and precisely identified. The wall in fact is dissolved in the garden.

Still Life

Very common among the Greeks, who called them *xenia*, or 'guests' presents', were small pictures of still-life. They were abundant in Pompeian painting of the second 'style' and were usually of good quality.

Whether painted or done in mosaic, these pictures reveal originality in tackling the problems of space, and they define it by using more than one plane, or by perspective tricks. As time goes on and the need for spatial experiment diminishes, other aspects come to the fore: naturalism, skilful lighting, great care in composition and, above all, dexterity in the orchestration of colour. Every now and then this skill results in tonal contrasts or in bright splashes of colour, and the impressionistic technique invests these with an atmosphere and a life that was rarely achieved in more ambitious works. This also applies to the representation of animals: the mosaic of the cat with a bird in its mouth (fig 167) at Pompeii, belonging to the second century BC, exists in several other versions. One is from the second century AD, another is from the age of Severus; and through them we can follow the stages by which the problem of space was resolved. We possess, too, various versions of the mosaic of the doves (fig 168)—a very common motif, derived from a famous mosaic by Sosos. Egypt, again, is evoked by scenes of water fowl in swamps amid Nilotic flora (figs 170, 171) and perhaps also by the scene of the heron being attacked by a cobra (fig 134). It is not mainly the search for chromatic effects or for agreeably decorative colour-contrasts which inspires the painters of such scenes, but a fondness for realistic portrayal of the animal kingdom. Even the various pictures of deep-sea fish (fig 169 is an example) display not only a purely pictorial merit but also a genuine talent for representing animals, with the result that zoologists can identify them today.

A large group of paintings goes by the name of 'small' *genre* pictures, and they are so freshly seen that in some cases (for example fig 122) their impressionistic technique gives them the spontaneity of a sketch. Another series of paintings is concerned with actors, theatrical scenes and concerts (*e.g.* figs 114, 115, 116, 144, 145) and is of value for the history of the antique theatre. In some cases, however, such as the two mosaics signed by Dioskurides of Samos (one of which is illustrated in fig 144) which are technically very accomplished, we possess real milestones in Hellenistic painting. But the theatre and Dionysus, its tutelary deity, are almost always present in the paintings and, even more, in the decorations of the Roman period—either as simple masks or faces, or as figures in the Dionysiac rites.

Caricature, as we find it in paintings at Rome and Pompeii, is also of Hellenistic origin, and Alexandria is usually regarded as the birthplace of certain little scenes in which the actors are pygmies and the landscape 'Egyptian', with local colour supplied by the flora and fauna. These motifs became popular and we find them again in later mosaics (*e.g.* fig 176) of the second century AD. In other pictures, the comic element lies in the situation (*e.g.* fig 150) rather than in the representation of figures deformed by nature (fig 151) or by the caricaturist himself.

Hellenistic Tradition and Roman Taste

In practice, therefore, 'Pompeian' painting and the Roman painting of the same period include all types; and this enormous heritage of paintings and pictures, of friezes and isolated motifs, provides us with a panorama in which we can follow all artistic trends from late Hellenism until almost the end of the first century AD and, in part, even further— academic neo-classical painting, impressionistic, tonal painting, and the kind which is usually called plastico-architectonic. Not infrequently we can see conflicts between invention and execution, between Hellenistic tradition and Roman taste. Thus on the one hand there are the higher currents of art which may follow the great Hellenistic tradition or veer more towards Neo-Attic classicism, and side by side with them the more original features detectible in certain landscapes, still-lifes and portraits; while on the other hand, there is evidence of a rivulet of 'popular' Roman painting—in shop-signs or in pictures from *lararia*, the parts of the Roman house where tutelary deities were kept. One example is the fragment showing Bacchus near a hill with vine-pergolas, which has been identified as Vesuvius (fig 123). The language of provincial Hellenism has become, in Italy, a popular dialect in which pictures of daily life are spontaneously created, and here the dialect itself becomes the language, as it does in figs 124 and 125, or in the watch-dog that appears in various mosaics (*e.g.* fig 175).

Portraiture

The painted portrait is a separate subject; unlike the portrait in sculpture, it is poorly represented on Italian soil. One at Pompeii, which stands out compared with the ordinary type such as the so-called 'Poetess', is the portrait of Terentius Neo and his wife (fig 138). It is remarkable for the robustness of its realism and for its impressionistic colour-contrasts—features which link it to the more 'popular' type of Pompeian painting. Broadly speaking, its formal characteristics, too, are very similar to those of a great series of portraits on wood (or occasionally on linen) which were included in the wrappings of mummies in Egypt. These are usually called Fayûm portraits—though improperly, for they have been found not only in the oasis of that name but throughout the Nile valley. Their origin lies in the time of the Pharaohs, when custom required the coffin to bear a portrait of its occupant; but their place is in the Graeco-Roman tradition. About six hundred examples are known, ranging in date from the Flavian era to the end of the fourth century AD. They are dated less on stylistic grounds than by such features as the way the women's hair is worn and the shape of the men's beards. The merit of various contemporary examples from the same area is remarkably diverse. In the first and second centuries AD individual realism usually predominates; later on, we find an increasing tendency towards abstract stylisation which culminates in the hieratic majesty of certain examples from the age of Constantine. Some specimens from the first period are given in figs 139–141.

To aristocratic art belongs another class of portraits—precious as regards its materials and its miniaturist's technique. This group is not numerous and belongs to the category of 'gilded glass'. This term derives from the technical basis that links these portraits with those in which the design is drawn on gold between two sheets of glass. In the latter the symbols and episodes are for the most part Christian, and they were found set in the lime which sealed the compartments in the catacombs, where they served as recognition marks for relatives. In the case of the portraits this was a highly refined art, even if the persons represented were sometimes less than aristocratic in appearance; but in the portrait on the glass at Arezzo (fig. 142)—a genuine painting on account of its poly-chromy which is further heightened by the purple stripe that falls from the right shoulder across the robe—the almost pained look in the sunken eyes imparts a certain nobility to the haggard face with its oddly-shaped brow Such plastic synthetism, rich in shading, makes this (with others in the same group) a typical example of the art of portraiture in the third century AD. Other portraits in the same technique occur in the following century.

Mosaics

Mosaic is an art of Hellenistic origin, but it enjoyed immense popularity throughout the Roman world. In various technical forms it was used from the very moment of its introduction to Italy for the decoration of pavements, and only much later was it applied on a large scale to the decoration of walls. *Opus tessellatum* was composed of little square or rectangular pieces of stone called *tesserae*, coloured differently from the stone in which they were set, and so arranged as to form a geometrical decoration. At first it was used to form a frame for the *emblema*, a central area with a design which might be a real picture (hence our previous references to mosaics) worked, as the most finished examples were, in *opus vermiculatum*. This name derives from the fact that variously-shaped little pieces of coloured stone were laid in serpentine lines (see for example the detail of the mosaic of the Battle of Issus in. fig 143). But as early as the end of the first century BC we find examples of 'carpet' mosaic, *i.e.* a type in which the pattern is continuous. There gradually emerged a scheme of decoration based on geometrical figures in various combinations: and in the larger designs that resulted, from the second century AD onwards, isolated motifs or figures were introduced. By that time, however, the design of pavements with a central *emblema* was being modified so as to give almost the whole area of the pavement to the *emblema*. In the second century AD we often meet with compositions in which the background is white, the figures black and the internal lines on them white. While Hellenistic mosaics, which derived from painting, used very small *tesserae*, Roman work achieved its own mode of expression by using larger ones and by emphasizing the joints in the mortar. Side by side with the coloured marbles and other fine-grained stones we find pieces of vitreous paste employed to create particular nuances. Throughout the Roman Empire, from Britain to the Mediterranean, from Asia to Iberia, mosaic pavements were very common. Yet it is chiefly in the non-Italian provinces that examples are most abundant today; they are often, moreover, of better quality than those that remain in Italy. They range from the cities of the East (the most remarkable series is at Antioch on the Orontes) to the cities of Africa (the mosaics of North Africa are of capital importance), from the villas of Italy and Sicily (figs 154, 155, 156, 157, 163, 172, 173) to villas north of the Alps (figs 158, 159). One of the most extensive sets and one of the most interesting from the point of view both of form and of content was excavated not many years ago in a very large villa at Piazza Armerina in Sicily (a few examples are illustrated in figs 160–162). These mosaics show various pictorial trends which still further complicate some controversial theories. Their date, especially, is uncertain, but it runs from the end of the third century AD into the fourth; and their relationship with the mosaics of North Africa is so very close that African craftsmen may perhaps have made them.

A further technique is that of *opus sectile*—a form of inlay, done with slabs of stone or marble of various colours, either cut into geometrical shapes or else shaped so as to form features in scenes containing figures. We possess many examples of the use of *opus sectile* for geometrical and ornamental pavements; in the later period especially such inlay work was used to exploit the contrasts between gaudy colours. Examples of its use for figures, which as a rule were placed on walls, are rarer. It is not possible to illustrate any of the pictures forming part of the decoration of the Basilica of Junius Bassus (from the first half of the fourth century AD) where the figure-scenes rival painting by the way in which their colour-schemes are based on divisionism, *i.e.* a system by which the colours are placed flatly side by side. For an example of this type of pictorial decoration we can turn, once more, to Pompeii (figs 164–166). There, for the presentation of Dionysiac scenes (derived from that Romano-Hellenistic repertory we know so well from the art of the early Empire and especially from decorative reliefs) a more restricted and delicate palette is used, with a design almost devoid of modelling.

Conclusion

It will be clear from many indications given above and from some of the examples illustrated that Roman painting consists of more than the kind called 'Pompeian'. But, alas, the Roman paintings of Central Italy, which exist in a fragmentary way in tombs and on the walls of ruined buildings, are not easy of access for photography. They exist, moreover, in a discontinuous series and there is often no agreement among authorities as regards their dating. To acquire a real understanding of Roman art one must have recourse to sculpture and above all to those historical reliefs whose solemn air reveals the 'official' trends in figurative art.

3

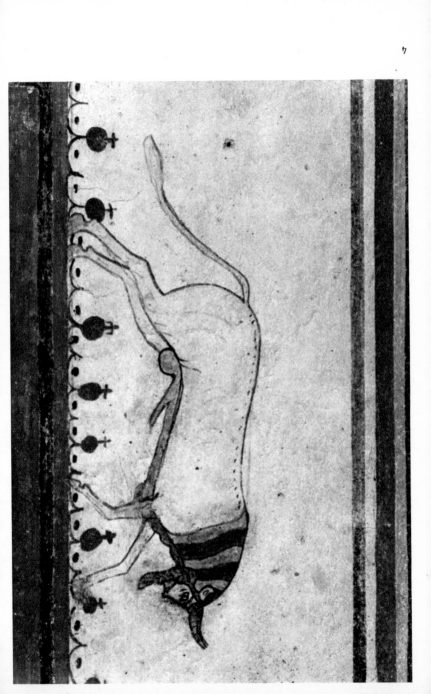

13

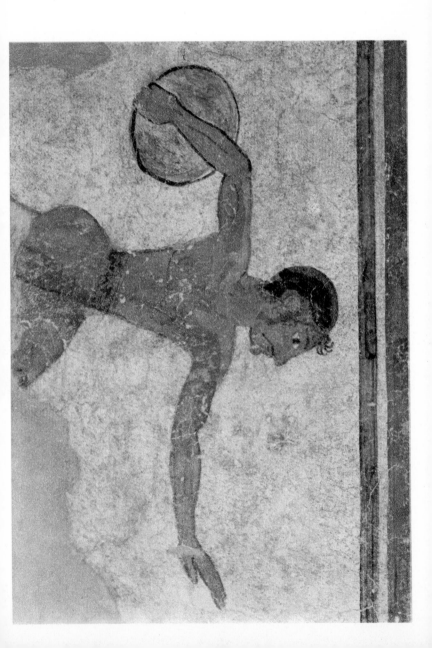

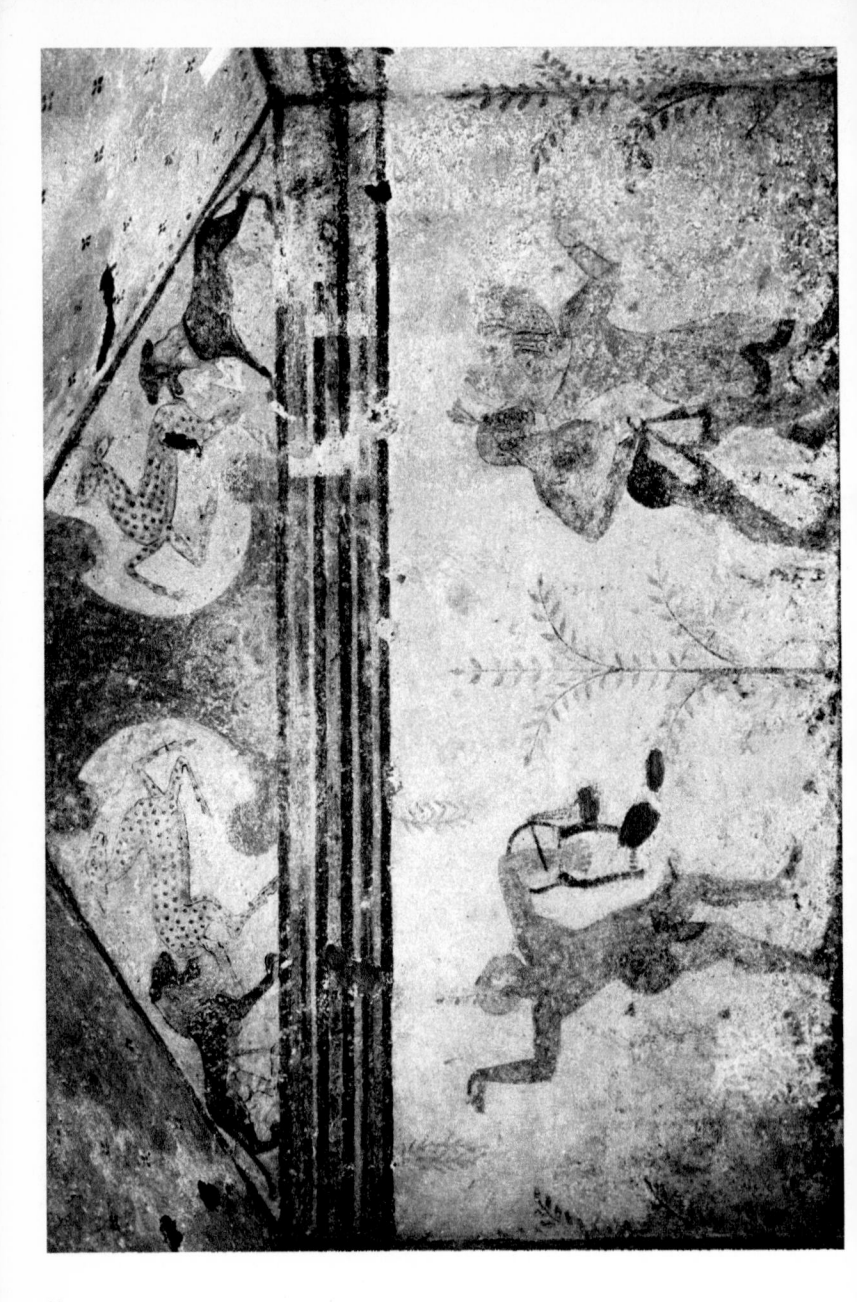

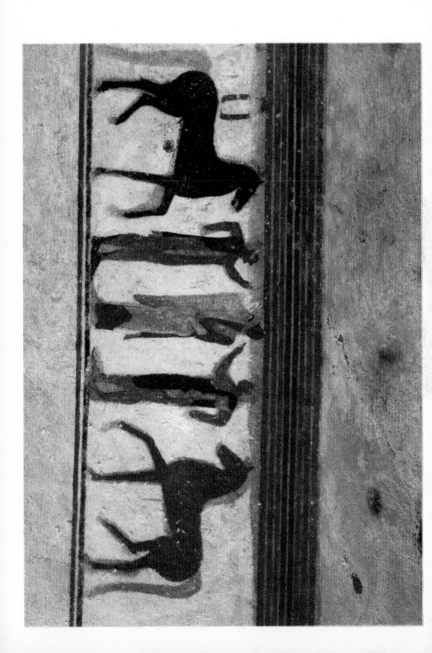

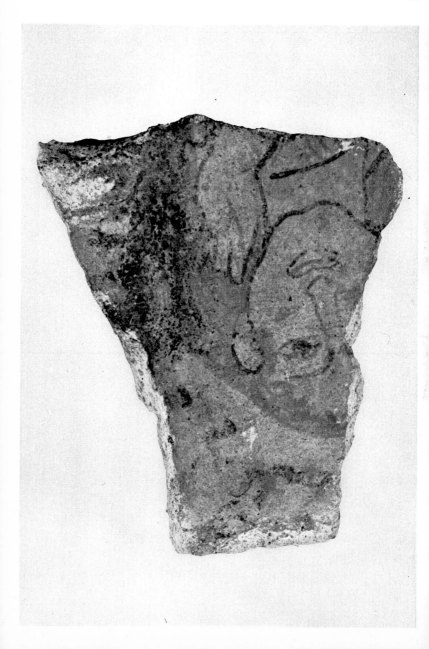

36

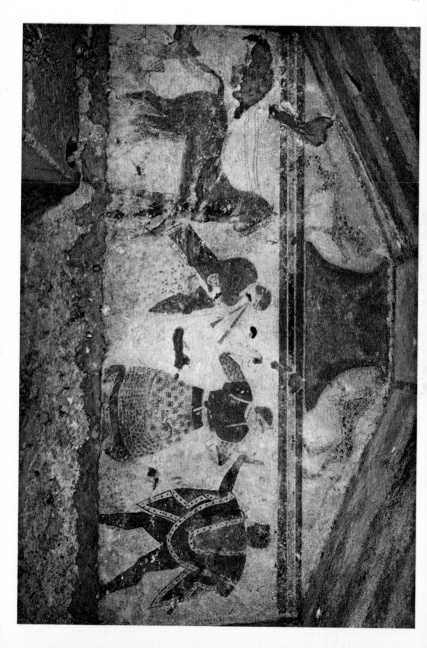

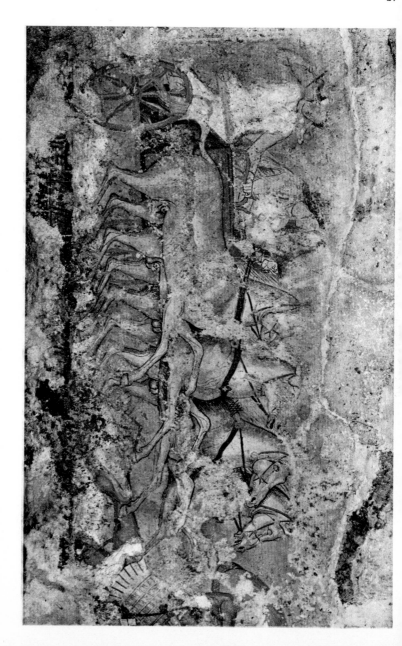

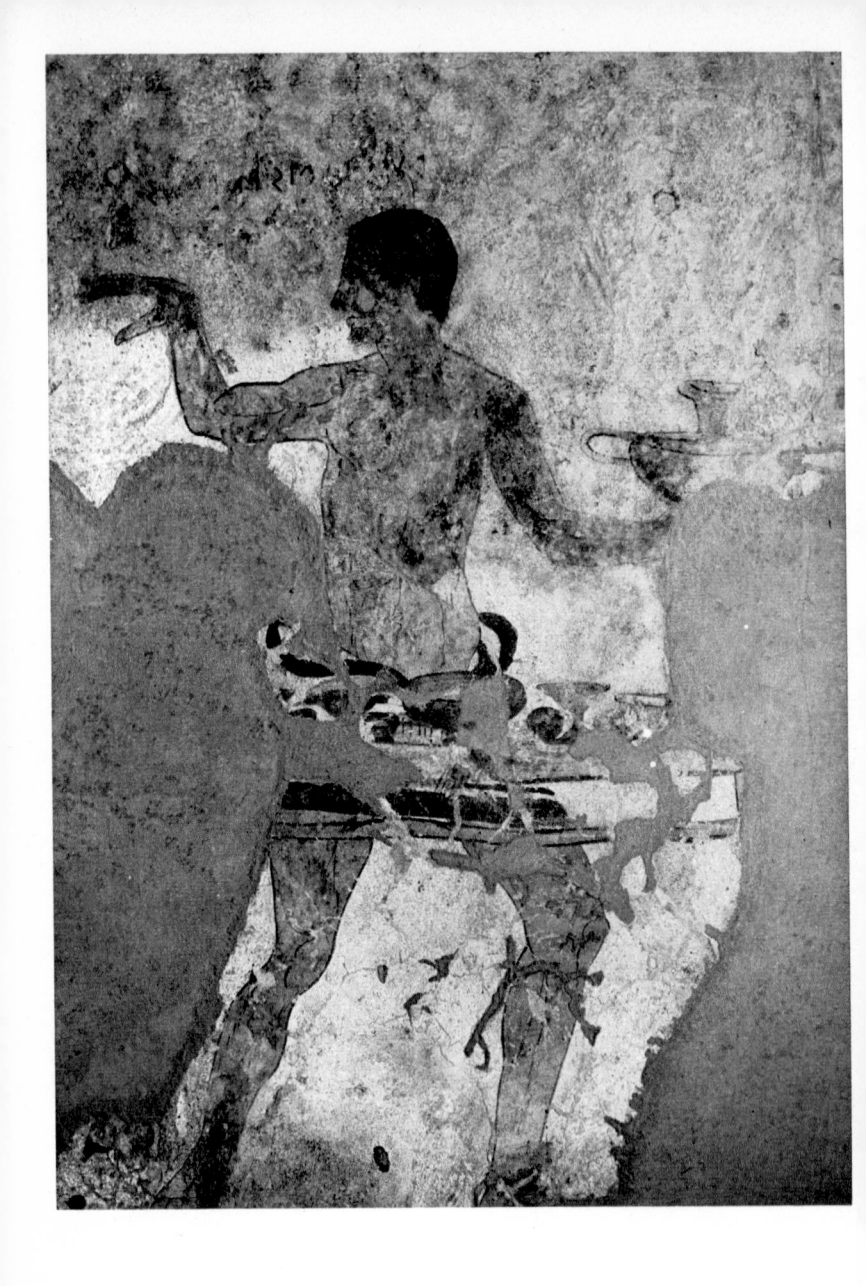

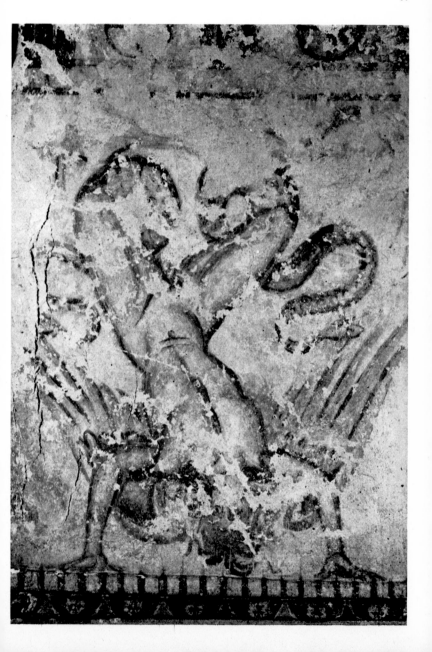

82

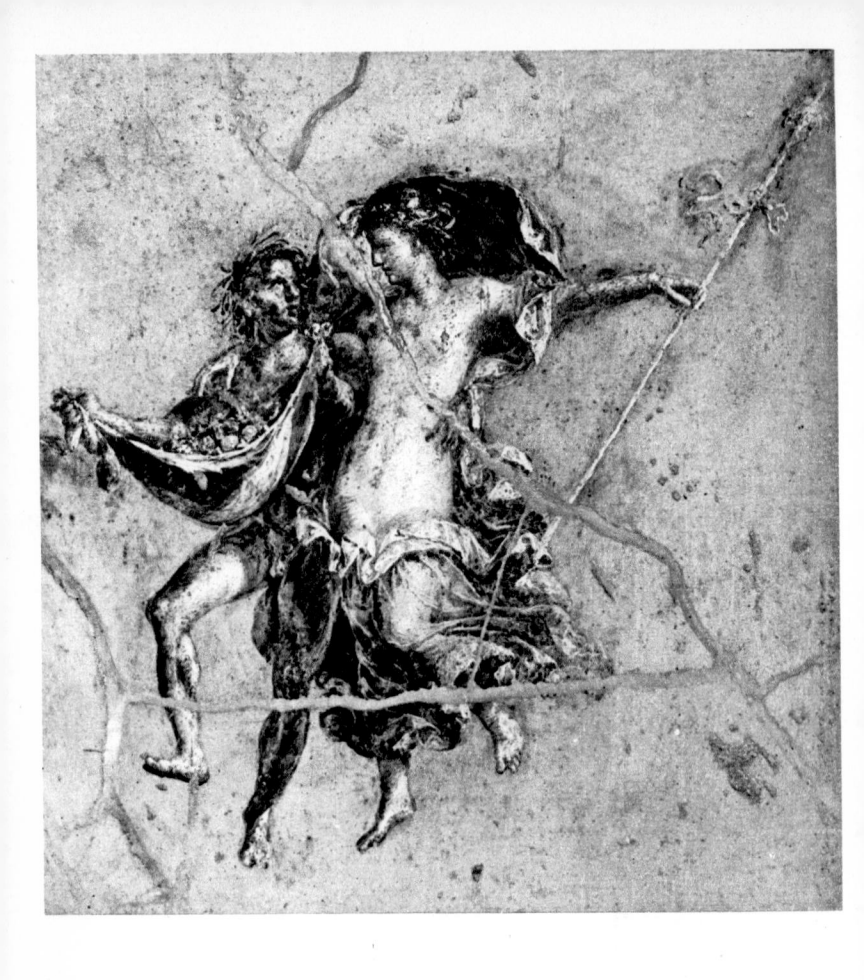

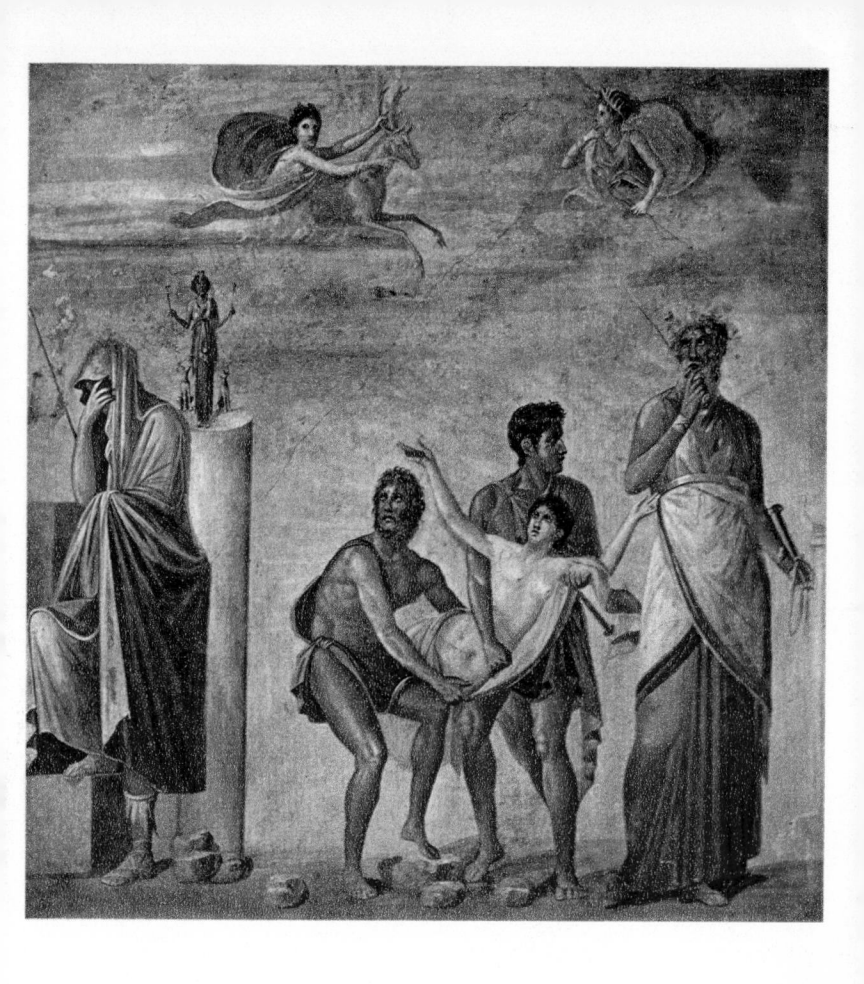

93

116

148

149

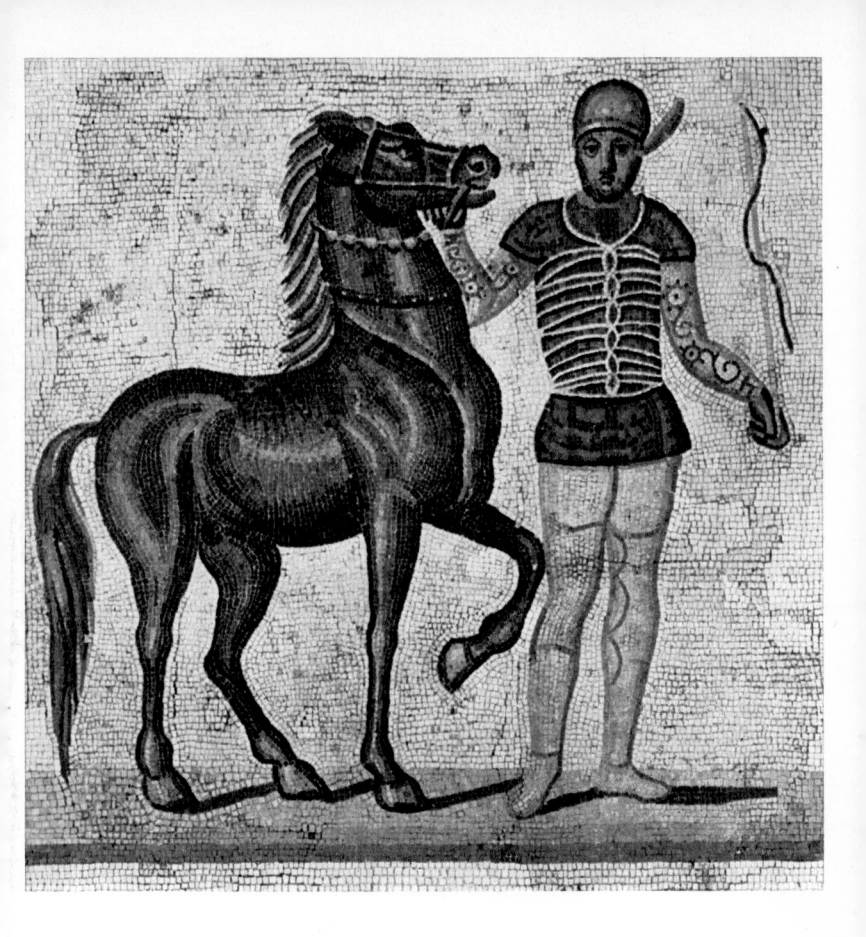

173